St. Cloud State Hockey: Guts, Goals and Glo
By Marty Mjelleli with Sean LaFavor

Printed in the United States of America

ISBN#: 978-0-615-93515-7
Library of Congress Control Number: 2013922980

Disclaimer:
This is not an official publication of St. Cloud State University, which bears no responsibility for any claims or actions related to this publication. Permission to use university trademarks has been granted by St. Cloud State University.

Personalities interviewed:
Jim Gravel, Dave Reichel, Morris Kurtz, Vic Brodt, Craig Dahl, Bill Prout, Brandon Sampair, Scott Meyer, Mark Hartigan, Andy Lundbohm, Bob Motzko, Joe Jensen, Matt Hartman, Casey Borer, Dan Kronick, David Carlisle, Ryan Lasch, Jon Ammerman, Aaron Marvin, Mick Hatten, Ben Hanowski, Dr. Earl Potter III, Garrett Raboin, Kirk Olson, Clay Matvick, Pierre McGuire, Jeff Passolt, Lou Nanne, Doug Johnson, Patrick Reusse, Bret Hedican, Matt Hendricks, Mark Parrish, Matt Cullen, Bill Frantti, Tom Nelson, Charles Basch

Publications:
2008-09 WCHA Men's Yearbook; 2013-14 NCAA Men's Ice Hockey Record Book; Various SCSU Men's Hockey Media Guides;
Iron Men: How Seven Imports from Ore Country Forged the Greatest Forgotten Season in Minnesota Hockey History, by Jayson Hron (Historically Inclined, jaysonhron.wordpress.com, Feb. 29, 2012)
Frozen Perfection: The 1962 St. Cloud State Huskies, by Jayson Hron (Minnesota Hockey Magazine, Oct. 28, 2013)
Frozen Memories, Celebrating a Century of Minnesota Hockey, by Ross Bernstein;
More...Frozen Memories, Celebrating a Century of Minnesota Hockey, by Ross Bernstein
A Tiff About Travel is put in perspective, by Mark Scherber (New York Times, March 20, 2002)
We Can't Hear You: The Story of the Children of Yost, by Michael Florek (Michigan Daily, May 31, 2010)
Ducks Prospect Lasch takes long way home, by Eric Stephens (Orange County Register, July 12, 2012)
All Hail the King, by Loren Nelson (MN Hockey Hub, 2011)
Roe makes his mark on hockey history books in Minnesota, by Reed S. Albers (Fairfax Times (Va.), March 16, 2011)
Drew LeBlanc's Comeback Lifts St. Cloud State Hockey, by Pat Borzi (The New York Times, Feb. 23, 2013)
St. Cloud faces challenge after major injuries, by Dan Myers (College Hockey News, Nov. 13, 2011)

Movies:
The History of St. Cloud State Division I History: Past. Present. Future, UTVS, Happy Elf Productions, 2007

Websites:
National Collegiate Hockey Conference http://www.nchchockey.com/
Western Collegiate Hockey Association http://wcha.com/
USCHO http://www.uscho.com/
St. Cloud State University http://stcloudstate.edu/
Hobey Baker Memorial Award Foundation http://www.hobeybakeraward.com/
Elite Prospects http://www.eliteprospects.com/
HockeyDB http://www.hockeydb.com/

Photos/Images:
USA Hockey, National Hockey League photos courtesy of: Atlanta Thrashers, Calgary Flames, Chicago Blackhawks, Colorado Avalanche, Columbus Blue Jackets, Detroit Red Wings, Edmonton Oilers, Nashville Predators, New York Rangers, Philadelphia Flyers, Pittsburgh Penguins, Toronto Maple Leafs, Vancouver Canucks, and Washington Capitals. Boston Bruins- Steve Babineau , Carolina Hurricanes-Gregg Forwerck, Minnesota Wild-Bruce Kluckholn, Montreal Canadiens-Bob Fisher, St. Cloud State Archives, Neil Andersen, Brace Hemmelgarn, Adam Hammer, Jan Korsgaard, BSU Photo Services, University of Minnesota Athletics, Gustavus Athletic Department, Princeton Office of Athletic Communications, SPX Sports, St. Cloud State University, Western Collegiate Hockey Association and WCHA Final Five, International Ice Hockey Federation, Hobey Baker Award, National Collegiate Hockey Conference, Front Cover and Interior Design by Jeff Lorenzen

To Everyone that has made Husky Hockey a Success

...Past, Present and Future

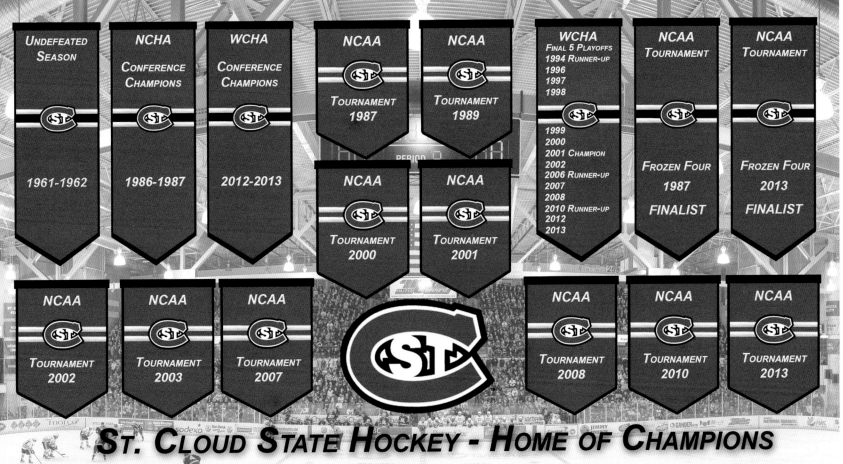

UNDEFEATED SEASON

1961-1962

NCHA CONFERENCE CHAMPIONS

1986-1987

WCHA CONFERENCE CHAMPIONS

2012-2013

NCAA TOURNAMENT 1987

NCAA TOURNAMENT 1989

NCAA TOURNAMENT 2000

NCAA TOURNAMENT 2001

WCHA FINAL 5 PLAYOFFS
1994 RUNNER-UP
1996
1997
1998

1999
2000
2001 CHAMPION
2002
2006 RUNNER-UP
2007
2008
2010 RUNNER-UP
2012
2013

NCAA TOURNAMENT
FROZEN FOUR 1987 FINALIST

NCAA TOURNAMENT
FROZEN FOUR 2013 FINALIST

NCAA TOURNAMENT 2002

NCAA TOURNAMENT 2003

NCAA TOURNAMENT 2007

NCAA TOURNAMENT 2008

NCAA TOURNAMENT 2010

NCAA TOURNAMENT 2013

ST. CLOUD STATE HOCKEY - HOME OF CHAMPIONS

McDONALD RINK

"St. Cloud State University not only provides another Division I hockey opportunity for kids in Minnesota, it also gives these student-athletes a chance at life success by teaching each player the importance of academics."
Bret Hedican, two-time USA Olympian and Stanley Cup Champion

"I am very thankful to SCSU for allowing me the opportunity to compete at the highest level, and in my opinion, play in the best league in all of college hockey. Throughout my four years I made great friendships with not only my teammates but also the community. One of Coach Dahl's teaching points was the importance of work ethic and why it's so valuable. The term "work ethic" is the foundation of Husky Hockey and that of the community in which they play. For this reason success has and will continue to follow."
Matt Hendricks, 2000 Mr. Hockey Finalist and NHL standout of the Nashville Predators

"No institution did more for collegiate hockey in the 30s and 40s than St. Cloud."
John Mariucci, the Godfather of Minnesota Hockey

"After a tour of the rink with assistant coach Tom Serratore, we went to Garvey Commons for lunch. I hadn't been on campus for more than three hours and to his amazement I committed right there on the spot to play for SCSU. I just knew; it felt like home and I knew this was where I wanted to be."
Mark Parrish, All-American, USA Olympian, and former NHL star of the Minnesota Wild

"It was more for philosophical reasons that I went there (SCSU), and that year went fast for me. Basically, that was one of the most enjoyable years I ever spent in hockey; it was fun."
Herb Brooks, 1980 Miracle on Ice, USA Olympic and former SCSU coach

"I wanted to go to a school that would give me the opportunity to play a lot so I could develop my skills. Playing on the big ice sheet allowed me to work on my skating. SCSU had everything that helped me get to the next level."
Matt Cullen, Stanley Cup Champion and NHL player of more than 1,000 games

The community of St. Cloud takes great pride in SCSU hockey. Our students show up every night, the turnout on the road is incredible, the applause and the noise they provide makes it an honor to represent them. They are loud and proud and they should be! We have accomplished a lot this year as a program.
Drew LeBlanc, 2013 Hobey Baker Award Winner

Foundations (1931-1986)

St. Cloud State University was founded in 1869 as St. Cloud Normal School, with the purpose of training high school graduates to be teachers. The very earliest hockey teams at SCSU date back to the turn of the 20th century, in 1898, though not much is known about the teams that represented the school in those years and for unknown reasons the team ceased playing in 1901.

The program was reborn in 1931, though by then the school was referred to as the St. Cloud State Teachers College, and its hockey team called the Pedagogues. Ralph Theisen had the honor of coaching the school's first hockey team that season, and while it didn't have much success on the ice in Theisen's lone season at the helm, finishing with a 1-7 record, the school's hockey program was back, this time for good.

Ludwig Andolsek took over as head coach beginning in the program's second season, serving in that capacity from 1932 to 1935, and was also the team's standout goaltender his first season before ceding the cage to future U.S. Hockey Hall of Famer Frank Brimsek. Andolsek, a Slovenian immigrant who grew up in Chisolm, liberally recruited players from Northern Minnesota's Iron Range, primarily Eveleth — where he himself skated for the town's junior college only a few years prior. These skilled recruits helped the team to a 42-4-1 record over his three seasons as coach. One of those recruits, Brimsek, came to campus in 1933-34 and quickly became the program's first star. Five years after his lone season in St. Cloud, Brimsek won both the Calder Trophy as the NHL's top rookie and Vezina Trophy as its best goaltender in 1938-39, ending that season backstopping the Boston Bruins to their first of two Stanley Cup championships in three seasons, both with Brimsek playing starring roles.

The Pedagogues, with a lineup laden with Iron Rangers that included Brimsek as well as future head coach Roland Vandell on defense, went 7-1-1 in that glorious 1933-34 season and were invited to the AAU's Midwestern Postseason Tournament in Chicago, while their neighbors to the south — coach Frank Pond's University of Minnesota squad — were not. Andolsek and President George Selke had tried repeatedly that season to schedule a game with the Golden Gophers, with good reason to believe that, with Brimsek on their side, they could beat the two-time defending Big Ten champions.

Early in the season, a powerful club from the University of Manitoba made its way through the state and swept a pair of weekend games against the Gophers in Minneapolis before stopping in St. Cloud on their way back north. In what turned out to be the first "huge" game in the fledgling program's history, Brimsek and Co. sent the Manitobans on their way with a 3-2 loss, snapping the Canadians' 17-game winning streak. Still, the Gophers could not be swayed to take on the Pedagogues, and the two teams never met that season, though the U of M's refusal was a source of some resentment for the Peds and their supporters, and the seeds of a heated rivalry were sewn.

St. Cloud was one of eight teams invited to the AAU postseason tournament that March, and the Pedagogues dispatched a pair of Chicago clubs, the Baby Ruth Cardinals and Pabst Blue Ribbons, to earn a spot in the championship game on March 18, 1934. Waiting for them was Eveleth Junior College, the club that Brimsek and most of the Peds' key players had competed for prior to coming to the Granite City. Because so many of the Peds' stars in those early years followed their coach to St. Cloud from the Iron Range school, Eveleth Junior College was one of SCSU's first big rivals, and perhaps no meeting between the two institutions matched the magnitude of that title game in 1934. St. Cloud scored five goals in the first period and another early in the second to take a 6-0 lead, but Eveleth came storming back for an eventual 8-6 victory. The Peds may have had a more talented starting five (and no goaltender in the land rivaled Brimsek), but it was Eveleth's depth that was the undoing for St. Cloud's Iron Men that weekend, as the team's five regulars very rarely left the ice for a breather in any of the three games in four days.

Andolsek brought in another crop of Eveleth Jaycees imports in 1934-35, his final season as the school's coach. One of those Iron Rangers was netminder Sam LoPresti, who played two seasons in the National Hockey League with the Chicago Black Hawks and still holds NHL records for shots faced and saved in a

EARLY 1970s

1969

LATE 1980s

1950s

SCSU HOCKEY

1930s

BEFORE THE ZAMBONI

1935

single game, stopping 80 of 83 attempts in a 3-2 loss to Brimsek's Bruins on March 4, 1941. Both Brimsek and LoPresti were later inducted into the U.S. Hockey Hall of Fame in 1973, and Brimsek gained entry into the Hockey Hall of Fame in Toronto in 1966 — thus far the only former SCSU player to achieve that feat.

Andolsek's club that final season earned an automatic bid to the 1935 AAU Minnesota State Tournament by virtue of its impressive performance in the Midwest tourney the year prior. They won all four games at the state tournament to once again secure a trip to Chicago, only now it was to compete for a national championship. This time they fell to the Baby Ruths in the semifinals and returned home with a third-place finish. With that, Andolsek graduated and resigned his post, returning to the Iron Range to take an education job with the federal government, ending one of the more remarkable periods in the program's history. The school cycled through three different coaches in the ensuing three seasons before George Lynch took the job in 1938 and guided the program for the next four years until it was suspended during World War II.

When the war ended and play resumed, former standout defenseman Roland Vandell returned to campus as head coach. Eager to have the school play against the finest competition available, he initiated many of the school's future rivalries, scheduling the first games against North Dakota, Michigan Tech and in-state opponents Minnesota-Duluth and Bemidji State.

Vandell got his signature win in 1948 when the Huskies won the St. Paul Winter Carnival championship by beating St. Olaf College, 5-4, in overtime of the title game of a tournament that also included strong clubs from the Universities of St. Thomas and St. John's. Leading that St. Cloud outfit in 1947-48 was captain Sergio Gambucci, a U.S. Hockey Hall of Fame inductee in 1996 who led the team in points for two seasons. Although Vandell had some success in the early years of his regime, the 1951-52 squad under his watch went 0-6 and there was real talk of shuttering the program. But with new coach George Martin in charge of things the following winter, the Huskies had one of their best seasons in years, posting an 8-3 mark in Martin's only season as coach.

Future SCSU President Brendan J. McDonald spent one season behind the bench in 1953-54, before Jim Baxter, who was also a player, guided the club to very solid 7-1 and 11-3-1 records in 1954-55 and '55-56. Baxter had a dizzying 33 goals in '55-56 and finished the season with 57 total points — easily a single-season school record at the time, one that stood for 31 years. The 45 points for Leo Goslin, Baxter's teammate that year, would have been a new school record if not for his coach's exceptional on-ice performance. During one incredible game against Augsburg that winter, Goslin had five goals and five assists (on five Baxter goals), giving him single-game records for goals, assists and points that he still shares today. His 27 assists that year stood as the record until Dave Reichel had 30 in 1977-78.

Jack Wink took over as the team's new leader in 1956-57 and coached the team (called the Huskies since 1952) for more than a decade. Wink, who also coached St. Cloud State College's football team, led the team to a remarkable undefeated 11-0-0 season in 1961-62. That team was led by a top forward line from the Twin Cities metro area: sophomore Henry "Skeeter" Hawkinson from Wayzata, a speedy, fierce competitor who led the Huskies with 16 goals and 19 points that year; and Minneapolis natives Ed Noble, a senior captain, and Phil Gens. Dale Carmichael shared goaltending duties with Rod Pickett, a junior from Baudette who played with the University of North Dakota freshmen team before transferring to St. Cloud after one year in Grand Forks and never lost a game in two seasons with the Huskies. Helping to persuade him to make that move was fellow Baudette native Bill Fritsinger. One of the highlights of that special season was a 4-3 win on the outdoor home ice against in-state powerhouse Bemidji State (the only team to beat the Huskies the season prior) during St. Cloud State College's Sno Days winter carnival on a frigid afternoon on Jan. 27, 1962. The Huskies finished off the perfect record with another win in Bemidji on Feb. 10 before tying a team of alumni in an exhibition contest.

The program may have been riding high in the early 1960s, but it won only a single game in each of the 1966-67 and 1967-68 campaigns, at which point Wink's stint as coach came to a close. Charles Basch replaced him and coached the program for the next 16 seasons from 1968-69 to 1983-84, compiling a 181-193-7 record. His 181 victories were a school record when he retired and ranked second in the program's history entering the 2013-14 season, 19 more than current coach Bob Motzko but well shy of Craig Dahl's 338 wins.

1961-62: The Undefeated Season

**Coach Jack Wink guided the Huskies to a perfect 11-0 record in 1961-62.
That team was inducted into the St. Cloud State Athletic Hall of Fame in 2004.**

Wink's team went a combined 6-42 in his final three seasons as coach, and Basch didn't fair much better with a 2-18 record his first season in 1968-69. St. Cloud was only marginally better (7-10) in his second season, and were up and down for most of his tenure — the program's best season in the 1970s was in 1973-74, when it etched a 15-6-2 mark into the record books. His teams mostly played clubs that today compete in the contemporary MIAC and WIAC — and of course Bemidji State and Mankato State — but occasionally they ventured further to play teams outside Minnesota and Wisconsin. In his first season the Huskies played four games against Lakehead University from Thunder Bay, Ontario; in the early '70s the University of Illinois-Chicago and Lake Forest College were frequent foes, including a trip to the Windy City to play those institutions to begin the 1970-71 schedule.

One of Basch's star players in the late '70s was Dave Reichel, now the color commentator on SCSU hockey broadcasts for KNSI Radio, who led the Huskies in points all three seasons he spent with the program from 1976-77 to 1978-79. When he finished his career, Reichel was the school's all-time leader in goals, assists and points (65, 73 and 138, respectively). Dave and his father, Jerry Reichel, who played for the program from 1952-53 to 1954-55 (player/coach Jim Baxter's first year at the college), were both inducted into the SCSU Athletic Hall of Fame together in 1991. "It was a thrill watching my dad read his letter notifying him of his induction," Reichel recalls. "We still remain the only father-son duo to receive that honor."

Two of Reichel's teammates in his final two years at SCSU both made serious runs at breaking those records immediately after he was gone. Steve Martinson piled up 133 points in his Huskies career, falling just five short of Reichel's standard, but he finished as the program's most prolific goal scorer (69). He also finished with a school-record 279 penalty minutes, a mark that still stands today as of the beginning of the 2013-14 season. He went on to a professional career that included 49 games in the NHL with the Detroit Red Wings, Montreal Canadiens and Minnesota North Stars. When Martinson retired as a player he took up coaching, and as the 2013-14 season began he was embarking on his second season behind the bench of the Central Hockey League's Allen Americans.

Martinson's running mate during his four seasons (1977-78 to 1980-81) was Jeff Passolt, who finished his career second on the all-time points list (136) and came up one goal short of his classmate with 68. Passolt went into television after college and has spent the past 30-plus years as one of Minnesota's most recognizable media personalities, first as a sports anchor then as a news anchor on local network affiliates.

Basch coached seven All-Americans in his stint as coach: Minneapolis native Ronald Gordon, a goaltender who earned the honor in 1969-70; Hibbing native Paul Oberstar (1970-71); and Roseville's John Fiztsimmons, who capped his senior year in 1972-73 as the first player in school history with 100 or more points (103, 47 goals and 56 assists). Crookston native Pat Sullivan was an All-American twice, in 1973-74 and '74-75, as was Reichel, who came to St. Cloud from Hopkins and took the honor in both 1977-78 and '78-79, when he recorded 51 and 52 points, respectively. Rory Eidsness was Basch's goaltender in the school's first season in the NCHA when the Fargo native was named an All-American, while defenseman Dan Pratt of Minneapolis manned the blue line for that team and joined Eidsness on the All-America squad. Basch's lengthy tenure as coach was marked by two very important developments in the program's history: the arrival of a long-overdue indoor playing surface for the team; and the formation of the Northern Collegiate Hockey Association.

For the first five decades of the program's history, St. Cloud depended on the outdoor elements for its home ice. The school's teams played on Lake George downtown in the early 1930s before moving to an outdoor rink located on campus, across the street from Eastman Hall, on the site where Brown Hall currently sits, during Lud Andolsek's term as coach. That remained the home rink until 1959 when Brown Hall was built and opened its doors for classes, at which time the team moved to another outdoor rink just south of University Ave., near where the Halenbeck Hall Fieldhouse now stands. When Halenbeck opened in 1964, that's where players on the hockey team dressed before practices and games.

In those decades of using outdoor ice, if it wasn't cold enough or if it was too cold, or there was more snow than the players could keep shoveled off the ice surface, they simply didn't play. By the early '60s, even many of the incoming freshmen from the Twin Cities and elsewhere were accustomed to playing their high school hockey on indoor, well-cared-for, temperature-controlled sheets of ice. The St. Cloud teams usually couldn't begin their seasons until the weather allowed them enough cold weather and time to create a proper ice surface, while rival clubs with indoor sheets got big head starts. As *Star Tribune* columnist

BILL KORFHAGE

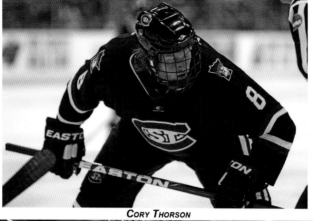

CORY THORSON

CHRIS ANDERSON

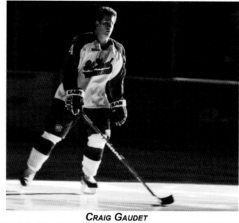

CRAIG GAUDET

DAVID CARLISLE

SCSU SWEEPS MINNESOTA STATE 2012

DAVID EDDY

DAVE IANNAZZO

MIKE HAJOSTEK

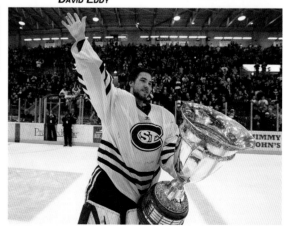

RYAN FARAGHER

(and former *St. Cloud Times* scribe) Pat Reusse noted in a February 2013 piece: "(St. Cloud's) ability to play a full home schedule was determined by when it got cold in central Minnesota and how long it stayed that way." Finally, in 1972, the first indoor ice sheet was installed at the Municipal Athletic Complex, and the Huskies (as well as St. John's University, numerous high school and youth programs in the area) had their indoor rink. They played at the MAC until construction was completed on the National Hockey Center in December 1989.

Basch was instrumental in the school finally succeeding in its long quest for indoor ice and also for making sure the Huskies were included when the NCHA was formed. He was also very popular with most of the Huskies who played for him. "Charlie was fun to play for, had a great sense of humor and a real laid-back coaching style. Also one of the nicest guys you will ever meet," recalled Jim Gravel, who played from 1977 to 1981 and led the team with 47 points (23 goals, 24 assists) as a senior that final season, 1980-81, the team's first in the "unofficial" NCHA. Gravel, a teammate of Reichel, Martinson and Passolt, had 51 goals and 101 points in his SCSU career, one of only six members of the school's "Century Club" of 100 or more points when he graduated.

St. Cloud State was a founding member of the Northern Collegiate Hockey Association, which formally came into existence on June 1, 1980. It consisted of six teams formerly competing in two now-defunct leagues, the International College Hockey Association and the Western Intercollegiate Hockey Association: SCSU, Bemidji State, Mankato State, UW-Eau Claire, UW-River Falls and UW-Superior. The NCHA, initially a Division II organization, began play unofficially in 1980-81 but the teams played unbalanced schedules, and 1981-82 is recognized as the new league's first official season. The whole league moved to Division III when D-II was discontinued for eight years from 1985 to 1992. Bemidji State was the dominant NCHA program during the Huskies' time in the conference, winning or sharing the regular season title the first five years of St. Cloud State's involvement. The Beavers captured a pair of national championships in 1984 (Division II, in Joel Otto's final year with the program) and 1986 (as a Division III program). They were also second at the D-II tournament in '83, losing the final to Rochester Institute of Technology; and at the D-III tourney in '85, again losing to RIT.

John Bergo was one of Basch's go-to players in his final seasons at the helm in the early '80s, earning All-NCHA honors in both his junior and senior year, including a nod to the First Team to cap his career in 1983-84. He eclipsed both Martinson's career goals mark with 76 tallies between 1980-81 and '83-84, and Reichel's record for most points (Bergo finished with 145). When Basch retired following the 1983-84 season, John Perpich was hired to replace him on an interim basis. Perpich played for Herb Brooks at the University of Minnesota and was a defenseman on the first NCAA championship team in Golden Gophers history as a senior in 1973-74, then was an assistant under Brooks during the school's third national title in 1978-79. He was an assistant coach for Team USA at the 1983 World Junior Championships in Leningrad, then head coach for the Under-20 team at the tournament the following winter in Sweden.

Perpich, known as a hockey tactician much like his mentor (and successor at SCSU), coached the Huskies for only two seasons and posted a solid 30-24-4 record, highlighted by a second-place NCHA finish his first year in '84-85. He left to become the head coach at Ferris State in April 1986 and later served as an NHL assistant coach for six seasons with the Washington Capitals and Los Angeles Kings, including for the Barry Melrose-led L.A. squad that featured Wayne Gretzky and lost to the Montreal Canadiens in the 1993 Stanley Cup Final.

His departure coincided with a push from St. Cloud State to realize John Mariucci's wish and become the state's third Division I program. To get there, the school enlisted the help of an American hockey icon.

GREG HAGEN

JASE WESLOSKY

JOHN DONOVAN, MARK REICHEL, GARY STEFANO, STEVE MARTINSON, DOUG RANDOLPH, KEVIN CLUNIS, DAVE ROOS 1980

DAN KRONICK

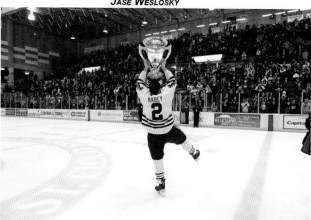

JARROD RABEY

KONRAD REEDER

AARON BROCKLEHURST

VIC BRODT

JIMMY MURRAY

JEFF PASSOLT

Building Respect (1986-1994)

The first time Craig Dahl spoke with Herb Brooks, the American coaching legend was looking for a house sitter, not an assistant coach. It was the summer of 1980, just months after Brooks orchestrated what many view as the greatest upset in sports history, the Americans' "Miracle on Ice" victory at the Lake Placid Olympics when a group of college kids beat the Soviet juggernaut and claimed gold medals. Their paths converged because Brooks, whose family lived in a house near Turtle Lake in Shoreview, had just taken a job to coach Davos in Switzerland's top league and was getting ready to move to Europe for the season. He needed someone trustworthy to watch his home, and Dahl had just accepted his first coaching job to take over the program at Bethel College, in nearby Arden Hills, and needed a place to live.

As Dahl tells it now, Brooks called him up "out of the blue" one day to broach the subject, and at first he wasn't sure whether to believe that Herb Brooks, perhaps the most famous man in America in the aftermath of the Olympic triumph, was actually calling him or if a friend was pulling a prank. But when Brooks mentioned having recruited Dahl's brother, Ross, to play for him at Minnesota, he was convinced. It was obviously a perfect fit, and Dahl agreed to watch the Brooks' home for the season.

Herb spent only one season coaching Davos before returning to coach the NHL's New York Rangers the following summer, at which point Dahl moved into an apartment in the area. But by then he had befriended Herb's son, Danny, who was in high school at the time, going skiing with him in the winter and hanging out together in the summer months, and he eventually became close with the entire family, often going to New York to see Brooks in action with the Rangers.

Dahl coached the Royals for five years before moving on himself to take over the program at Wisconsin-River Falls for the 1985-86 season. The following summer, Brooks, who'd been dismissed by the Rangers in January that year, got in touch with his former tenant and asked for his thoughts on taking the coaching job at St. Cloud State. "I asked him, 'Why would you want to go coach a Division III team,'" Dahl recalls, incredulous at the time that the coaching legend would want to go from coaching an NHL team in New York City to taking over a little-known D-III school in central Minnesota. "'Well, they're trying to take it to D-I,' he said, and he asked if I'd like to go with him to check things out."

So the two headed for St. Cloud, met with then-President Brendan J. McDonald and Bill Radovich, then-Vice President of administration ("the money guy," as Dahl called him) and then-Athletic Director Morris Kurtz. They toured the university and checked out the Municipal Athletic Complex rink, where the Huskies played at that time. Dahl was not initially impressed.

"We got together after the meeting and he asked what I thought. I told him 'I don't think they have any idea what it's going to take (to move the program to Division I)," Dahl said. The MAC was not a building worthy of a D-I program, Dahl told him. It was too small, the locker rooms were inadequate and he didn't think it would be worth the hassle. "So he told them, 'Thanks, but I'm going to have to respectfully decline.'"

The university brass didn't take 'no' for an answer, and continued their pursuit of Brooks, and eventually both he and Dahl reconsidered. "A week later, he calls and says 'They agreed to make some improvements (to the MAC) and they're going to try to get some legislation for a new rink. Let's go back up and take another visit,'" Dahl recalls. After that trip, Brooks had seen and heard enough to be convinced, but he needed to make sure Dahl was on board. "I've got to have you with me. I need you to handle scheduling, recruiting, academics and all that stuff," Brooks told Dahl. "I'll go if you go," was Dahl's response. And the rest, the saying goes, is history.

A buzz filled the air after Brooks announced he'd take over as the team's head coach, as St. Cloud realized it potentially had its own 'Miracle on Ice' in the making. His involvement with the program brought it an unprecedented credibility. After going 16-11-2 in John Perpich's final season, the Huskies finished 25-10-1 in 1986-87 and were co-winners of the NCHA regular season title with Mankato State, the first time Bemidji State failed to win at least a share of the

AARON MARVIN

ADAM COOLE

ANDREW PROCHNO

BRANDON BURRELL

BILLY HENGEN

T.J. McELROY

BILL LUND

BRENT BORGEN

BOB MOTZKO

championship in the league's first five years of existence. That St. Cloud State team in 1986-87 set 45 school records and stands as one of the most important in the program's history on many levels. "Herb had a way of obtaining the most from his players; he made us feel that we couldn't lose. He didn't tell us that, we just felt it," remembers Vic Brodt, one of the holdovers from the Division III years who competed in the program's fledgling Division I years. He was a freshman in '86-87.

The team earned a No. 1 seed in the Division III NCAA Tournament and swept the Salem State Vikings in a best-of-three quarterfinal series, earning a spot in the Final Four in Plattsburgh, N.Y. The dream of a national championship was shattered following a 5-2 loss to Oswego State in the semifinals, but the team responded with a 6-4 victory over Bemidji State — the NCHA playoff champs — in the consolation game to bring home a third-place finish.

That proved to be Brooks' only season behind the Huskies' bench, as North Stars general manager Lou Nanne hired him to once again lead an NHL outfit, and Dahl took over the SCSU coaching job. Joining him that season was Mike Eaves, a former North Stars player who in 2013-14 was beginning his 12th season in charge of the University of Wisconsin men's program as the Badgers started play in the new Big Ten Conference. Brooks' departure was bittersweet, but as then-Athletic Director Morris Kurtz notes, "Herb was the foundation of our (Division I) program. What he did in one year, no one else could have accomplished in a lifetime."

One of the biggest advocates for SCSU's progress was John Mariucci, known as Minnesota's "Godfather of Hockey" for his advocacy of the amateur game in the state. As legend has it, Mariucci almost came to St. Cloud for his college playing career but was stolen away by the Gophers with a $100 scholarship. As Brooks' mentor, Mariucci urged the 1980 Olympic hero to fill the head coaching position at SCSU, thinking it'd be a good way for Brooks to give back to the sport and help grow the college game within the state. In 1987-88, SCSU competed for the first time as a Division I program, and Mariucci's wish was fulfilled. Reflecting on his lone season with the Huskies, Brooks later lamented: "That was one of the most enjoyable years I ever spent in hockey; it was fun."

Brooks commuted to St. Cloud from the Twin Cities for practices and games that season and helped some with recruiting initially while Dahl handled the day-to-day details of the operation. But the head coach spent many hours at the capitol in St. Paul, lobbying the legislature for a new arena. Brooks was then, and remains today, a hockey icon in the U.S., but particularly in his home state, and his efforts to get a new arena for SCSU carried weight no other person was likely capable of carrying. Also working in the school's favor was that Rudy Perpich, Minnesota's governor at the time, was a big sports fan and generally sympathetic to projects that involved funding for recreational facilities. Near the end of 1987 Brooks' hard work paid off and funding was secured. Groundbreaking on the new arena, which cost $9.5 million and was to include two Olympic-sized ice sheets, began in the fall of 1988, about the same time Dahl and the Huskies were beginning their second season in Division I. "Having Herb's 'name' was a huge deal (for getting the new arena built)," recalls Dahl. "It was just the perfect tsunami of the right people in the right places at the right time."

While many college hockey arenas since then were built much more lavishly than the NHC, Dahl notes it was one of the nicest arenas in the WCHA in St. Cloud State's earliest years in the league. Minnesota had played in Williams Arena (the hockey side of which was renamed Mariucci Arena in 1985) since 1949, and while "The Barn" was beloved by Gophers fans, many of its idiosyncrasies made it a less than ideal place to actually watch hockey; Denver played in a building built in the early 1940s and originally used by the U.S. Navy as a drill hall — in northern Idaho. DU Arena, as it became known, was broken down, relocated and put back together on the Denver campus, where Magness Arena now stands, in the late '40s; Colorado College had played in the Broadmoor World Arena since 1938, and no other WCHA rink used at that time had been built since 1974 (Northern Michigan's Lakeview Arena).

In the early part of 1989-90, their third season as a Division I independent, the Huskies played a lot of road games as they waited for the National Hockey Center to be completed, and following a sweep of Michigan Tech in Houghton to open the schedule, they didn't have much to show for it. At home, playing the program's final games at the MAC, St. Cloud went 1-6 and its overall record stood at 4-13-1 when finally, on the weekend of Dec. 16-17, 1989, the National Hockey Center was ready. The Huskies christened their new home with a sweep of Northern Michigan, with 5-4 and 4-2 decisions, respectively, and went 13-6-1

JASON GOULET

2013 NCAA MIDWEST REGION CHAMPIONS

TAYLOR JOHNSON

NICK OLIVER

2001 FINAL FIVE CHAMPIONS

RYAN PECKSKAMP

2006 SCSU TEAM COLORADO SPRINGS

NICK OSLUND

RYAN LAMERE

SCSU PRESIDENT EARL POTTER

ETHAN PROW

JOE KEARNEY

the rest of the way. They finished that season playing 15 of 20 games on home ice, including 11 in a row following a trip to Marquette to play NMU the first weekend of January. Included in that stretch was a 6-5 win at the NHC on Jan. 9 over Wisconsin, which went on to win the national championship that spring.

The following season, the Huskies transition to Division I was complete, as St. Cloud State became the ninth member of the Western Collegiate Hockey Association — arguably the toughest conference, top to bottom, in NCAA hockey. Active WCHA members included: Colorado College, University of Denver, Michigan Tech University, University of Minnesota, University of Minnesota-Duluth, University of North Dakota, Northern Michigan University, and University of Wisconsin. "Joining the nation's top collegiate conference was the launching pad for community excitement and recruiting success as the Huskies proved worthy of the task." said Center Ice Club President and longtime fan, Bill Prout. It was a huge step for Dahl and his program. But as the new kids on the block, SCSU's real work had just begun.

St. Cloud State's evolution into a Division I program was relatively smooth. They often held their own against the tougher competition and even earned an NCAA tournament bid as an independent in 1988-89 — giving coaches something to boast about a little on the recruiting trail. Dahl's rosters in those early years were a mishmash, players initially brought in to play Division III hockey while his staff simultaneously recruited new players geared toward play at the higher level.

Blaine, MN native Mike Brodzinski was the last of SCSU's great players who never took the ice as a Division I athlete, and he finished his career tying John Bergo for the most goals in school history (76) and eclipsing Bergo's all-time points total by one, finishing with 146. As such, Brodzinski's name is forever etched atop the record books for St. Cloud State's pre-Division I era. Amazingly, he accumulated those totals in only three years with the program, transferring to SCSU after one season (and one game played) at the University of Minnesota in 1983-84.

Brodzinski looked like anything but a rookie in his debut, recording 20 goals and 34 points. His brother, Steve, joined the program the same year and finished his own outstanding career with 45 goals and 94 points (the two combined for 54 goals and 107 points in their final season). In catching up to Bergo's standards, Mike Brodzinski also set pre-Division-I era single-season records with 38 goals and 65 points as a senior in 1986-87 — the season Brooks roamed the Huskies bench with Dahl. He was named an All-American each of his final two seasons. Jonny Brodzinski, Mike's oldest son, was a freshman on the Huskies team that finally broke through to the NCAA Frozen Four in 2013, while a younger son, Michael, was a freshman for the Gophers in 2013-14. Both went to Blaine High School, the same place Mike and Steve played their prep hockey a generation before.

Herm Finnegan was one of the best of the "transition" Huskies, playing as a freshman on the Brooks team in '86-87 and leading the Huskies with 35 points as a sophomore in the maiden Division I voyage the next year. Vic Brodt was another, a classmate of Finnegan's who finished his career with one fewer point when the two graduated in 1990 (Finnegan had 114; Brodt, 113). Tray Tuomie came in as a freshman the same year and piled up 62 points in only two seasons before transferring to the University of Wisconsin.

With Brooks coaching the North Stars and Dahl now in charge, the Huskies played more that first season in Division I than any team before it in school history, and Dahl's charges performed admirably against the tougher competition with an 11-25-1 record. They played the Gophers for the first time in the U.S. Hockey Hall of Fame Game at Eveleth's Hippodrome on Oct. 3, 1987, and lost 6-0. SCSU improved dramatically to 19-16-2 in 1988-89 and earned the first Division I NCAA tournament bid in school history. The team traveled to Sault Ste. Marie, Mich., to play the defending national champions, Lake Superior State, and the Lakers swept the upstart Huskies with victories of 6-3 and 4-2, respectively.

Dahl, who went on to lead the program for 18 seasons and won more games than any coach before or since, admits it was a long uphill climb to get the program to a level where it could consistently compete with the likes Division I powers Minnesota, Wisconsin and North Dakota year in and year out. His primary focus in recruiting, he says, was going after kids with good character as well as elite hockey skills — kids who would work hard both on the ice and in the classroom. He and his staff diligently monitored their players' attendance, and if a hockey player skipped class, he didn't play during the weekend. "My

BRETT LIEVERS

SCSU TAKES THE ICE

GEORGE AWADA

DEAN WEASLER

RITCHIE LARSON

DICK BEAUDET

SENIORS OF 2008

DAN O'SHEA

KALLE KOSSILA

NIC DOWD

philosophy was if a kid goes to class, it's pretty unlikely that he won't pass." Still, it took a long time before the Huskies could "get" a player they recruited that was also fiercely sought after by those more established rivals. "I didn't think about failing. We knew it would be a challenge, but I never looked at it as something we couldn't do," Dahl said.

One of the Huskies' first "gets" in those early days was Saskatchewan-born Len Esau, who was drafted in the fifth round by the Toronto Maple Leafs in the summer of 1988 before beginning his freshman season at SCSU. He led the Huskies that season with 39 points — as a freshman defenseman. Esau played one more season in St. Cloud before beginning his professional career with the AHL's Newmarket Saints in 1990-91, and went on to play a handful of NHL games each with the Maple Leafs, Quebec Nordiques, Calgary Flames and Edmonton Oilers. He also played with Team Canada at the 1995 World Championships, earning a bronze medal.

Doc DelCastillo, who years later returned to his alma mater as an assistant coach, was also a freshman on that 1988-89 squad that played in the NCAA tournament as an independent. So was Bret Hedican, who played forward at North St. Paul High School before coming to St. Cloud State, but Dahl converted him to defense before the start of his first season. It seems that was a savvy move, as Hedican went on to play more than 1,000 NHL games with the St. Louis Blues, Vancouver Canucks, Florida Panthers, Carolina Hurricanes and Anaheim Ducks — as a defenseman. The Blues' 10th-round draft pick in 1988 went to the Stanley Cup Final with Vancouver in 1994, coming up one game short of a ring when his team lost in seven games to the Rangers — New York's first title since 1940. It took 12 years before Hedican returned to the Final, and this time it was his Hurricanes prevailing in seven games for the championship.

Hedican, in his third and final season at SCSU, became the first Husky named to the All-WCHA First Team, then bypassed his senior year to play with Team USA in preparation for the 1992 Olympic Games in Albertville, France. He represented his country four more times in his career, including another Olympics in Torino, Italy, in 2006 — before he and Matt Cullen helped the Hurricanes win the Stanley Cup later that spring.

While Hedican was preparing to represent his country, two of his former SCSU teammates were wrapping up the most offensively prolific careers in the program's history to that point. Jeff Saterdalen and Tim Hanus, a pair of highly-regarded recruits from the Minneapolis suburbs, combined for 151 goals and 351 points in their four years together with the program and occupied the top two spots of the program's record book in nearly every offensive category for a decade or more.

Saterdalen, a coach's son who played high school hockey for his father, Tom, at Bloomington Jefferson, was the first Husky to reach 100 assists in his career (101), and remained the only one until Ryan Lasch broke the record in 2009-10. Only Garrett Roe (the current record holder with 113, as of the start of the 2013-14 season) and Drew LeBlanc (105) have joined them in that exclusive club. Saterdalen, an eighth-round pick by the Islanders in 1987 before the start of his senior year with the Jaguars, also finished his career with the program's all-time records for goals, 78, which still ranks third; and points (179), which stood until Lasch wrapped up his career with 183. Hanus was also an NHL draft pick in 1987, going to the Nordiques in the seventh round before his senior year with the Minnetonka Skippers. He finished just shy of his classmate in goals (73), assists (99) and points (172) but still ranks in the top five in program history in all three.

Perhaps fittingly, the Huskies' first game as a member of the WCHA came against the Minnesota Golden Gophers, on Oct. 12, 1990, in front of 7,050 fans at the National Hockey Center, a new attendance record for the arena in its second year of service. The game ended in a 3-3 tie, lending hope that the Huskies were ready to compete in the toughest league in college hockey. They validated that impression with a home sweep of Colorado College the following weekend, and a pair of wins at UMD in mid-December. But the highlight of that first WCHA season came a week after that trip to Duluth when Northern Michigan visited the National Hockey Center. St. Cloud swept the Wildcats, who went on to win the WCHA regular season and playoff championships before winning the NCAA title with an epic 8-7, triple-overtime win over Boston University at the St. Paul Civic Center.

COLIN PETERS

P.J. LEPLER

GENO PARRISH

TONY GRUBA

BRETT HEDICAN   CRAIG DAHL   KRISTI YAMAGUCHI

CRAIG SHERMOEN

MATT HENDRICKS

GRANT CLAFTON

JOE REHKAMP

JOEY HOLKA

GARRETT MILAN

They finished fifth during their first trip through the league with an 18-19-4 mark that year, including sweeping all four games of the season series against Colorado College (the Huskies were 6-0 against CC to start their Division I era before the Tigers got their first win). But SCSU graduated a pair of key contributors to those early D-I efforts: Brian Cook led the Huskies with 31 assists and 50 points that season and finished his career with 48 goals, 76 assists (a new all-time record) and 124 points. Chris Scheid, meanwhile, joined Cook as one of only seven members of the program's "Century Club," wrapping up his career with 73 goals, 46 assists and 119 points. St. Cloud State won its first WCHA playoff game at North Dakota on March 1, 4-2, but were run over by a 10-2 score in Game 2 on Saturday and fell 7-4 in Game 3 on Sunday in Grand Forks.

The following season, 1991-92, Saterdalen and Hanus graduated, as did Mike O'Hara, a goaltender from Fullerton, Calif., who was the Huskies' workhorse for most of those first four Division I campaigns along with Craig Shermoen, though O'Hara ceded the starter's job that season to a freshman from Brandon, Manitoba. Grant Sjerven led a solid group of newcomers that year that were solid contributors immediately and served as the next major links in the chain that kept the program progressing forward. Sandy Gasseau was named to the WCHA All-Rookie Team that year, and fellow freshman blueliner Kelly Hultgren was later a two-time All-WCHA Second-Team honoree. Plymouth native Eric Johnson, another member of that rookie class, improved each season at SCSU and finished his career with 86 points.

Fred Knipscheer was St. Cloud's first NCAA First-Team All-American in 1992-93, when the junior blew away Saterdalen's single-season goals record by 10, with 34 (only Mark Hartigan has since scored more). His 60 points also topped Saterdalen's 57 three years earlier.

The Huskies took several very significant steps forward in 1993-94, easily their best since joining the WCHA, beginning in October in the second week of the season. After coming home from Michigan Tech having been swept by the league's "other" Huskies to open the schedule, St. Cloud beat the University of Minnesota Golden Gophers for the first time ever, 3-2, at a rockin' National Hockey Center on Oct. 29, 1993. They earned a 4-4 tie the next night in the first WCHA conference game at the new Mariucci Arena, and split the two-game rematch in March (including an 8-4 home win) to claim five of eight points. Hultgren was the rare defenseman to lead his team in points, with 37 in his junior year, as that Huskies team didn't boast any stars — Knipscheer had passed up his senior year to join the Boston Bruins, spending most of that year with their AHL affiliate in Providence; senior Tony Gruba had much better seasons in his previous two seasons but still chipped in a vital 10 goals and 27 points; freshman Dave Paradise would finish his career with 122 points when he closed the book on his Huskies career in 1997, third most in the Division I era at the time. He had 14 goals as a rookie that year, tied for second on the team, but SCSU's strength that year was its depth, not big names. Depth, and a home-ice advantage that helped them go 16-1-3 at the NHC.

The program posted its first winning season in league play with a 16-12-4 record, finishing higher in the standings (fourth place) than they ever had before. That meant they also hosted their first home playoff series, at the newly renamed Brendan J. McDonald Rink at the NHC. The Huskies promptly swept Minnesota-Duluth for the school's first trip to the WCHA Final Five, held at the Bradley Center in Milwaukee, and shocked the home fans there on Dave Holum's game-winning overtime goal for a thrilling 3-2 win over Wisconsin in a semifinal matchup. So on Saturday night, St. Cloud State found itself in the league's championship game the first time ever. Waiting for them were the Gophers, and after SCSU's first sustained success against them in the regular season, there was reason to believe they might come home with their first hardware.

Paradise opened the scoring for the Huskies 12:08 into the first period, but Brian Bonin answered only 28 seconds after that. Minnesota freshman Nick Checco and Gino Santerre traded goals in the second and neither team scored in the third, so the game went to overtime. Only a minute, 49 seconds into the extra session, Checco, Minnesota's Mr. Hockey at Bloomington Jefferson the year before, beat Sjerven and snuffed out the upset bid. The Huskies had lost 3-2, and the automatic NCAA berth that came with the WCHA title evaporated.

VICTORY 1986-87

MIKE O'CONNELL

JEFF SATERDALEN

JUSTIN FLETCHER

JOHN ETNIER

BIG SAVE AGAINST UND

STEVE HAATAJA

MARTY MJELLELI

RYAN FARAGHER

SENIORS OF 2011

DAVID CARLISLE

MIKE HASTINGS

A Giant Leap (1994-1999)

The St. Cloud State media guide is full of references to a proud, rich history of outstanding players and colorful personalities that came before the 1995-96 season, including a 6-foot-2 goaltender from Illinois who finished his career with a selection to the WCHA Final Five All-Tournament Team in 1994. With Grant Sjerven playing professionally in '94-95 the goaltending job was available, though it would not be for long. Brian Leitza was named to the WCHA All-Rookie squad that year and in 1998 graduated owning nearly every career goaltending record in the book. Nobody has come remotely close to his benchmark of 133 career games played — Mike O'Hara, at 98, is a distant second. Leitza's 66 career victories also provide a fairly comfortable margin over Scott Meyer, who won 47. The Huskies, paced by solid final seasons from Kelly Hultgren, Brett Lievers, Eric Johnson, Billy Lund and Sandy Gasseau, missed out on the WCHA Final Five that year, finishing fifth and earning home ice for a second straight year (Alaska-Anchorage had become the league's 10th team the season before), but were swept by North Dakota. Still, things were moving forward and the Huskies showed they belonged in the WCHA, though they had yet to claim a "signature" win, had no signature moment.

Of all the names that came before in the history of the SCSU men's hockey program, none have had the seismic impact of Matt Cullen and Mark Parrish. The two names are forever linked in the lore of Husky hockey — Cullen and Parrish; Parrish and Cullen. Both were among the state's 10 Mr. Hockey finalists as seniors that year, and both were blue-chip prospects that every college coach who cared about winning would have loved to have coming to play for him. And as it turned out, both were heading to St. Cloud to play for the Huskies.

Both came from high school programs in Minnesota that were wildly successful during their prep careers. Parrish played for two state championship teams at Bloomington Jefferson, including as a sophomore on the Jaguars team that rolled over everybody on the way to a perfect 28-0 record in 1992-93, their second title in a row. They won a third straight in 1993-94, this time beating Cullen's Moorhead Spuds in the final. The Jaguars went 25-1-1, and it was big news when they finally lost. Spanning the three consecutive championship seasons, Jefferson lost a total of three times — winning 79 and tying twice.

Meanwhile Cullen, playing for his father Terry, made it to the state tournament with Moorhead three consecutive years, and the Spuds made it to the championship game his junior and senior seasons. In 1994, Parrish's Jaguars finished off Moorhead's season in the final. Dave Spehar and Duluth East ended Jefferson's reign in the quarterfinals in 1995 with an emphatic 5-0 shutout, then won the first title in the Greyhounds history with a 5-3 win in the final, the third time in four years the Spuds were denied in the championship game.

Cullen led SCSU with 41 points as a freshman, one of the greatest seasons by a first-year player in school history, and was named to the WCHA All-Rookie Team. Following that first year, the Mighty Ducks of Anaheim took him 35th overall in the second round of the 1996 NHL Entry Draft, the highest a St. Cloud player had ever been selected. Parrish (who Colorado took with the 79th overall pick in the third round that summer) was nearly as good, ranking third on the team with 15 goals and finishing with 30 points, though the pair's gaudy stats didn't translate into a big win total. Senior Taj Melson tied with Dave Paradise for second on the team with 38 points and was named to the All-WCHA Third Team. Melson, a defenseman from Plymouth, graduated with 87 points, still second most ever among defenders in the school's Division I era.

The Huskies finished eighth in the standings (10-18-4 in league play) and headed to Denver for the first round of the playoffs. After a 3-1 Huskies win at the old DU Arena on Friday night, the Pioneers drew even with a 6-4 win of their own Saturday, setting the stage for a decisive Sunday showdown. Denver finished third in the WCHA that season but their record wasn't strong enough to bow out in the first round and still seriously expect to receive an NCAA bid, so both teams were fighting to continue their seasons. Leitza backstopped a 4-0 win for the Huskies, and it was on to the Final Five they went.

While the top two seeds, Colorado and Minnesota, respectively, had taken care of business, the other three series were upsets according the seeding. And so, St. Cloud squared off at the Bradley Center in Milwaukee against Michigan Tech in the play-in quarterfinal game the following Thursday. The Huskies

GARY HOUSEMAN

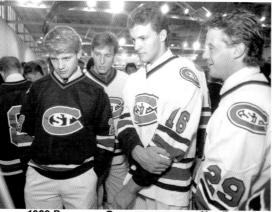

1989 PLAYERS AT GROUNDBREAKING FOR NEW RINK

KEITH ANDERSON

SAM ZABKOWICZ

FROZEN FOUR BOUND- 1987

MARK HARTIGAN   JON CULLEN

1947-48 WINTER CARNIVAL CHAMPIONS

RASMUS REIJOLA

TIM DALY

SENIORS OF 2010

from Houghton skated to a 4-3 overtime win, ending SCSU's upset run, then knocked off CC with a 4-3 win Friday before the Gophers finally dispatched Tech in the title game.

The dynamic duo stayed only two years on campus, both departing after the '96-97 season ended, but both definitely made those two years count. Cullen again led SCSU in points (45) and with 30 assists, and the Huskies had four players with 40 or more points that year: in addition to Cullen, junior Sacha Molin, an All-WCHA Third-Team honoree that year, tied with Paradise at 43 each, and Parrish had 42. Cullen was named to the All-WCHA Second Team and Parrish was named an NCAA West Second-Team All-American.

Leitza was again outstanding as a junior that year, while White Bear Lake's Scott Meyer, who would play a far greater role in the future, made his debut in one game of action after two seasons of junior hockey. St. Cloud's 23 wins overall and 18 WCHA victories both set new Division I-era records for the school, which finished third — only three points out of a tie for first — and hosted Northern Michigan for the first round of the playoffs. The Wildcats, who headed for the CCHA the following year, put a bow on their time in the WCHA by being swept at the National Hockey Center.

The Huskies headed to St. Paul to meet No. 2 seed Minnesota, co-winners with North Dakota of the MacNaughton Cup as WCHA regular season champs, in the late Friday semifinal of the last WCHA Final Five ever played at the St. Paul Civic Center. Both teams scored in the first period, but Molin, Cullen and Jason Goulet — a valuable but less heralded member of the sophomore class that season — found the back of the net in the second to give St. Cloud a 4-3 lead after two periods. The Gophers bombarded Leitza with 47 shots for the game, including 16 in a furious third period, but they could only get one of those by the junior netminder, and the game went to overtime.

In the extra time it was Mike Crowley, a teammate of Parrish on those Jaguars championship teams, who shoved home the winning goal. The WCHA Player of the Year and Hobey Baker finalist after tying for the league lead in points got a couple close-in whacks at a rebound to finally get one past Leitza, and again the Huskies came home empty. They lost to CC in the third-place game the next day, 6-0, and that was it for the Cullen/Parrish era. Four WCHA teams were given NCAA tournament bids on selection Sunday, but despite their most successful season since moving to Division I, the Huskies' resumé was not enough to secure one of them. North Dakota (after winning the Broadmoor Trophy with an OT win over the Gophers) went on to win the NCAA championship, but the league's third-place team was left home.

Cullen and Parrish were gone in 1997-98 — the former skating as a rookie with the Might Ducks while the latter joined the Western Hockey League's Seattle Thunderbirds, earning WHL First-Team All-Star honors. Parrish racked up 54 goals and 92 points in his one season of Canadian major junior hockey. The Huskies that returned still had enough talent to go 16-11-1 and finish fourth in the conference. Sophomore Matt Noga led the team with 37 points, and defenseman Josh DeWolf, a second-round pick of the Devils in 1996, led the defensemen that year with nine goals and 18 points. Senior Mike Maristuen bettered his entire three years combined leading up to that and finished second on the team with 31 points, including a team-best 16 goals. And anchoring it all was Leitza, who set new school records for games played by a goaltender (38) and wins in a season (22 — all of them). His 1,041 saves as a senior that year are still a program high.

Just before Christmas 1997, the Huskies gave their fans a long-awaited present, sweeping the Gophers for the first time in school history on Dec. 19-20. A month earlier, they went to Colorado Springs and gutted out a road sweep over a CC team that won 26 games that season. For their efforts, Leitza was named an All-WCHA Second-Team member, and Craig Dahl was the WCHA Coach of the Year.

St. Cloud needed all three games of their first-round series with Michigan Tech at the National Hockey Center to dispatch the MTU Huskies, and headed to Milwaukee for the last WCHA Final Five played at the Bradley Center. SCSU made it through the play-in game with a 5-4 win over Minnesota-Duluth but lost the semifinal the next night to North Dakota, the two-time MacNaughton Cup champs. On Saturday the Huskies fell in the third-place game, again losing to Colorado College, before the Wisconsin Badgers claimed the Broadmoor Trophy in front of the red-clad mob in Milwaukee later that night.

MIKE DOYLE

DALE CARMICHAEL

DEREK EASTMAN

ANDY LUNDBOHM

HERM FINNEGAN

MIKE BRODZINSKI MIKE VANNELLI

2005 HUSKIES IN ANCHORAGE

JAKE MORELAND

NATE HARDY

MATT NOGA

JOHN SWANSON

Noga led the Huskies in points for a second year in a row, but freshman Tyler Arnason, a Blackhawks draft pick and the son of former NHL winger Chuck Arnason, ended up second with 31 points (14 goals, 17 assists). He headlined a freshmen class that also included forward Nate DiCasmirro and defenseman Mike Pudlick, who played key roles on teams in years to come.

NCAA Bracketology (1999-2005)

Despite many very talented players and good teams that had worn the cardinal and black, no Huskies Division I team had returned to the NCAA tournament since Craig Dahl's second-year independent broke through in 1988-89. The team 10 years later that finished seventh in the WCHA included Brandon Sampair, a Mr. Hockey finalist as a senior at Hill-Murray in 1996-97 who wasn't much of a factor as a freshman but took huge strides every year after and soon emerged as one of the Huskies' key leaders. Other talent-rich recruiting classes filtered in thereafter forming the nucleus of the program's first championship contenders: Tyler Arnason was very much a factor as a freshman and was second on the team with 31 points in 1998-99. He and Mike Pudlick played key roles early in their careers, as did Mark Hartigan, who also joined the team that year but didn't make his debut until the following season.

St. Cloud State's 10th season in the WCHA marked the first for an old NCHA foe, as Mankato State once again gave the league 10 teams. The Huskies boasted perhaps their deepest offensive attack ever and once again had an elite goaltender, and all that finally proved enough to put an end to the team's run of frustration. The Huskies were relatively young but they were good — really good. Sophomores Arnason and Nate DiCasmirro finished in the top two slots on the points table — Arnason leading the team with 30 assists while both had 19 goals. And Hartigan found the back of the net a team-high 22 times and had 42 points, the same total as Sampair. Twice before in their Division I history, SCSU had four players with 40 or more points, but in 1999-00, they also had two finish with 30 — Ryan Malone and Duvie Westcott.

The NCAA tournament selection committee sent them to the East Regional in Albany, N.Y., for a game against Boston University and freshman sensation Rick DiPietro, the skilled puck-handling goaltender who went to the Islanders with the first overall pick in that summer's draft. The '99-00 season was the first as a starter for junior Scott Meyer, who played very sparingly in three previous seasons with the program (11 games) before finally claiming his spot as the full-time starter. "I thought I was working hard, but (Dahl) made me realize I was not," Meyer said. "He made me earn every minute of playing time and that helped me play better than I ever imagined."

Meyer was a revelation that year and recorded seven shutouts, still a school record, and SCSU finished third in the WCHA, equaling at the time its best finish in the league in program history. And they did it in style, sweeping a home-and-home series with the Gophers on the final weekend of the regular season to secure the final four points, with junior Keith Anderson scoring on a breakaway in overtime for a 4-3 win at the National Hockey Center to finish the job in Saturday's game on March 4. They hosted UMD for the first round of the playoffs, and after a slip up Friday night secured a hard-fought best-of-three series win in what turned out to be Mike Sertich's final games as coach of the Bulldogs after 18 seasons. At the WCHA Final Five at the Target Center the following weekend, SCSU fell to the eventual national champions, North Dakota, before beating the Gophers for third place.

The season ended in Albany with a 5-3 loss to the Terriers on Saturday afternoon, March 25, at Pepsi Arena. Mike Pudlick scored the first SCSU goal in a Division I NCAA tournament game since 1988 at the 12:22 mark of the second period, but only after BU had scored three times in the first period, opening up a lead that was never seriously challenged. After the Huskies were eliminated Pudlick, an All-WCHA First-Team honoree from Blaine, signed shortly thereafter as an unrestricted free agent with the Los Angeles Kings — leaving the program and taking his booming slapshot with him. It didn't end exactly the way they wanted, but it was a season the program could be proud of — and one it could build on, setting the stage for the winningest season in school history in 2000-01.

With Meyer back for his senior year, as well as all four leading scorers from the NCAA tournament entry, expectations for the Huskies were higher than they'd ever been. That team featured eight future NHLers in Arnason, Hartigan, Meyer, Duvie Westcott, Matt Hendricks, Jeff Finger, Joe Motzko and Ryan

ANDY VICARI

BRIAN VOLPEI

BRETT BARTA

BILL FRITSINGER

MIKE & JONNY BRODZINSKI

CHRIS HEPP

CASEY BORER

HOCKEY WEST REGIONAL

2010 NCAA TOURNAMENT- ST. PAUL, MN

ROGER RUTTEN AND RON MUIR

BRET HEDICAN

Malone, who'd played 584 NHL games with the Penguins and Lightning as of the end of the 2012-13 season and played for Team USA at the 2010 Olympics in Vancouver. The son of long-time NHL scout Greg Malone highlighted yet another impressive crop of freshmen the year before that proved to be key contributors as sophomores: Malone and Motzko, as well as center Jon Cullen (Matt Cullen's cousin) and Derek Eastman — a defenseman from St. Paul's East Side that also produced Herb Brooks generations before him — who would score one of the most infamous goals in school history later that season. "The guys I played with were so talented and some of the third- and fourth-line guys are the ones still in the NHL," reminisces Meyer of that team his senior season. "They made you better every day and it was great playing with them."

The Huskies set new standards for most wins (31) and best winning percentage (.768), as well as fewest losses in a season (nine) — marks that have yet to be eclipsed. They also allowed the fewest goals any SCSU team has ever yielded (92), thanks in large part to the heroic efforts of Meyer, an NCAA West Second-Team All-American that year. In the middle of that magic season, the Huskies rattled off a nine-game winning streak that spanned more than a month from Dec. 9 to Jan. 20. As the season's end drew near, the possibility of the first MacNaughton Cup title as WCHA regular season champions loomed as a real possibility.

The Huskies did their part with a five-game winning streak to end the regular season, but heading into the final weekend's home-and-home set with the Golden Gophers, it was Minnesota who stood poised to win a share of the MacNaughton. League leader North Dakota, with 42 points and playing a non-conference series at Bemidji to end its schedule, stood four points ahead of the Gophers and had already clinched at least a tie for the championship, and SCSU went into the weekend with 36 points and a best-case scenario of finishing second.

Friday night at Mariucci Arena in Minneapolis, the Huskies quickly doused any Gophers title hopes. Jon Cullen registered a hat trick in the first period and the Huskies chased starting goaltender Adam Hauser with three more goals in the third period, cruising to a 6-1 win anchored by a 37-save effort from Meyer. The atmosphere Saturday night at the National Hockey Center was as electric as any in the building's history, and the result wasn't much different than Friday's. Arnason and Hartigan staked the Huskies to a 2-0 lead after 20 minutes of play, and Westcott made it 3-0 on a 5-on-3 power play about midway through the second. Duvie added a shorthanded marker in the third and Motzko got on the scoreboard as well. Meyer, as he had been all year, was outstanding in making 36 saves as SCSU more than satisfied the packed house that night with a 5-2 win — securing the No. 2 seed in the WCHA playoffs and just as important, designation as the home team when the two teams met two weeks later in the Final Five semifinals.

Both teams easily dispatched their respective foes in the first round of the WCHA Playoffs, the Huskies pounding Alaska-Anchorage by 5-1 and 8-2 decisions on home ice. That set the stage for the Friday-night semifinal against Minnesota on March 16, in front of more than 18,400 at the Xcel Energy Center in St. Paul — the first year the WCHA Final Five was held at the Wild's new state-of-the-art hockey palace. The Huskies played perhaps their best defensive game of the season, limiting the potent Gophers offense to only 23 shots, with Meyer stopping all of them. They also killed nine Minnesota power plays. Chris Purslow and Nate DiCasmirro scored 40 seconds apart early in the first period for the only goals St. Cloud needed, and Tyler Arnason added a shorthanded tally in the second that actually went through the net. Play continued for several seconds before officials were able to go back and review the play, only then realizing the shot had tore through the twine.

In the WCHA championship game for only the second time, and first since 1994, the Huskies faced Dean Blais' top-seeded North Dakota Fighting Sioux — the defending WCHA regular season and playoff champions, and the defending national champions — on St. Patrick's Day, amid a sea of green at the Xcel. It turned out to be one of the wildest title games in the WCHA Final Five's history. The Huskies led 4-1 after two periods on goals from Derek Eastman, Joe Motzko and a pair of tallies by Arnason, the eventual tournament MVP. Arnason completed a hat trick in the final period, but the Fighting Sioux roared back with four goals of their own (three in the final 5 minutes, 33 seconds) in the third. Defenseman Travis Roche — who three weeks later made his NHL debut with the Wild — scored the equalizer with only 11 seconds left and goaltender Andy Kollar pulled for an extra skater to make it 5-5. It might have been completely understandable if St. Cloud, facing one of the more intimidating squads in recent WCHA memory, withered in the overtime and allowed North Dakota to

TIM BORON

2013 "LOCKS OF LOVE" PARTICIPANTS

MIKE NOTERMANN

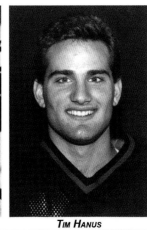

TIM HANUS

SCSU CHEERLEADERS

NATE WRIGHT

JIM GRAVEL

MITCH RYAN

JOHN BERGO

JARED FESTLER

TONY SCHMALZBAUER

GARRETT LARSON

complete the comeback — indeed, that was the expectation of many in attendance that night. "The atmosphere in the locker room was surprisingly calm after we gave up the three-goal lead," recalls Brandon Sampair, the Huskies senior captain that season. "We decided to go out in overtime and play like we had in the first 50 minutes of the game because we knew we had a talented team that could get chances in overtime."

Instead, the two teams played more than half a period of spirited, edge-of-your-seat hockey, and the Huskies actually outshot the Sioux 7-3 in the extra session, though Kevin Spiewak drilled a shot off the goalpost that nearly ended things in UND's favor. Instead, it was Eastman, the sophomore from St. Paul Johnson High, delivering St. Cloud State's first piece of major hardware in the Division I era. Eastman's slapshot at the 11:33 mark beat Kollar and found the back of the net for an apparent 6-5 victory. As the rest of the team came spilling over the boards of their bench to celebrate, several Sioux players appealed to the referees that Kollar had been interfered with. The play went to replay as the near-capacity crowd waited tensely. Replays showed that senior Ritchie Larson had indeed knocked Kollar to the ice, and that Eastman's perfectly-timed shot a moment later entered the net without a challenge from the junior goaltender. But much to the Sioux's dismay, the rules of the replay dictated that only the on-ice official could decide if contact was made with the goaltender (it most certainly was, and referee Mike Schmitt made no such ruling) — the only factor the replay booth could examine is whether Larson was in the crease when the puck entered the net. He was not, Schmitt signaled "Goal," and the Huskies again (officially) celebrated, triumphantly hoisting the Broadmoor Trophy as SCSU's first WCHA champions.

That earned the Huskies a No. 2 seed in the West Regional in Grand Rapids, Mich., which meant they needed only win a single game for their first trip to the NCAA Frozen Four ever. In those days, only 12 schools received NCAA tournament bids, split into two regionals of six with the top two seeds in each receiving first-round byes. In Grand Rapids, the Huskies awaited the winner of a first-round matchup between the Michigan Wolverines — enjoying somewhat of a home-ice advantage 130 miles away from their Ann Arbor campus — and upstart Mercyhurst College, the regular season and playoff champions of the Metro Atlantic Athletic Conference, from Erie, Pa. The Lakers played even, tied at 2-2, with Maize and Blue through the first 20 minutes, despite being outshot 21-7 in the first period, and even took a lead with a power-play goal in the third period before the Wolverines restored order and advanced with a 4-3 win, outshooting Mercyhurst 51-24.

The Wolverines were led that year by future NHL standouts Mike Cammalleri and Mike Komisarek, and a senior class that had won a national championship as freshmen in 1998. Michigan carried play and peppered Scott Meyer, putting the Huskies in a hole with two goals in the first period before Sampair and Cammalleri traded tallies in the second. With their backs against the wall, the third period was by far St. Cloud's best of the day, and Mark Hartigan scored on a power play only 1:24 in to cut the lead to 3-2. But it took Michigan only 2 minutes to re-establish a two-goal lead, and they advanced to the Frozen Four with a 4-3 win, despite another power-play tally by senior Keith Anderson with 5:08 to play. The Wolverines lost their NCAA semifinal to Boston College, setting up a rematch of the 2000 title game held in Providence between the Eagles and North Dakota, only this time BC prevailed, in overtime, to capture that program's first national championship since 1949.

Graduation and early departures hit the program hard that offseason, as the Huskies lost five seniors, including their captain, Sampair, and Meyer, their All-American netminder; and Arnason and Westcott, a pair Winnipeg natives, gave up their remaining eligibility to sign NHL contracts — Arnason with the team that drafted him, the Chicago Blackhawks, and Westcott as a free agent with the Columbus Blue Jackets. "We had a great mix of guys that knew their role on the team: the grinder, the scorer or the passers," Sampair recalls. "It was one of the few times in hockey when no one cared who scored, our goal was simple: win and have fun doing it."

One of the "scorers" Sampair spoke of had opportunities to leave that summer, but chose to come back for the WCHA's 50th anniversary season. Mark Hartigan and Arnason combined for 55 goals in 2000-01 (28 for Arnason, one more than Hartigan with 27), more than any other pair in a single season in history, so the Huskies would need to lean on the British Columbia native heavily in what turned out to be his final season. He proved to be up to the challenge.

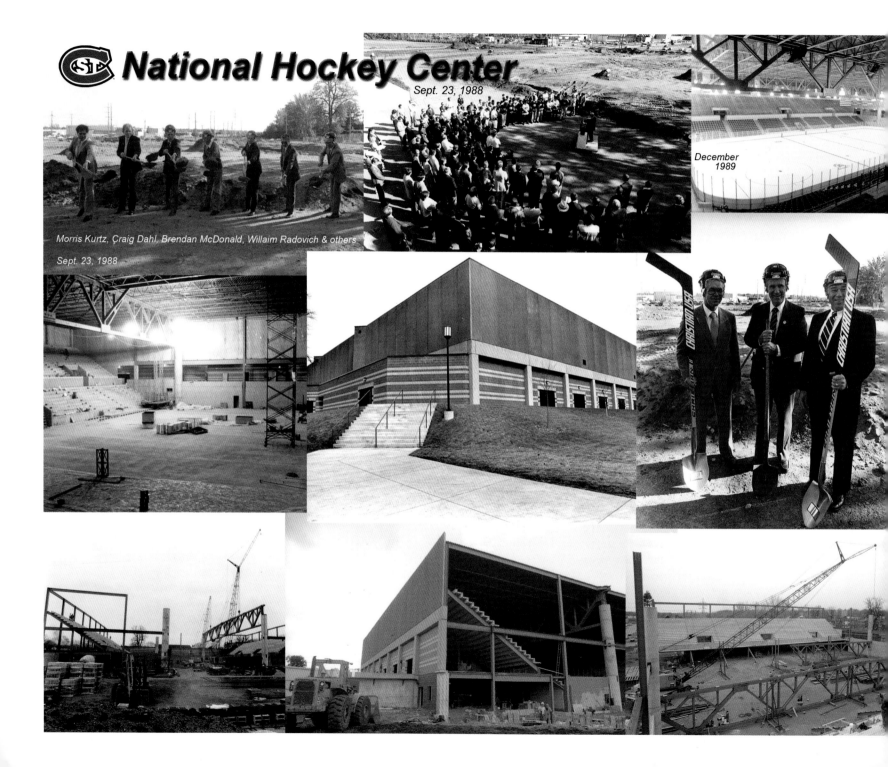

National Hockey Center

Sept. 23, 1988

December 1989

Morris Kurtz, Craig Dahl, Brendan McDonald, Willaim Radovich & others

Sept. 23, 1988

Hartigan, who played junior 'A' hockey in Weyburn, Saskatchewan, before coming to SCSU, outdid himself in 2001-02, re-writing the Huskies' single-season record books with 37 goals, 38 assists and 75 points in 42 games — all still the gold standard for the program (the 38 assists are even with Sampair's total the year prior and one more than Drew LeBlanc's 37 that led the nation in 2012-13). Included in that impressive resumé was a home game against Alaska-Anchorage on Feb. 15, 2002, when Hartigan scored four goals in the second period of a 7-4 win over the Seawolves.

Dean Weasler, who had been the Huskies' primary starter as a freshman in 1998-99, was back as a starter again as a senior after deferring to Meyer for two seasons, though junior Jake Moreland saw action in 17 games as well. The coaching staff had planned to redshirt the Rosemount native in 2000-01, realizing that with Meyer around they were pretty set in goal, while Weasler mended from injuries incurred his second year. But during a series at Colorado College in early February 2001, Meyer was sidelined with a concussion and Dahl turned to Weasler, asking if he'd be willing to give up his redshirt — and a future season of eligibility in the post-Meyer era — to help the team in the short term. He readily agreed.

Nate DiCasmirro was the top senior skater back in 2001-02, finishing second on the team with 33 assists and a career-high 50 points, tied for fifth most in school history at the time and tied for sixth now. Ryan Malone's role with the team grew in his junior year, as the Pittsburgh native and Penguins draft pick improved to 49 points (second on the team with 24 goals).

The Huskies started the season with nine consecutive wins, losing for the first time on a Saturday night against Colorado College on Nov. 10, 2001. They entered the weekend home series with the Tigers ranked No. 1 in the USCHO.com national poll and slipped to No. 3 when the next rankings came out. That was the only blemish on their schedule as they headed to Minneapolis for the Friday end of a home-and-home with the top-ranked Golden Gophers on Nov. 30, a meeting between the No. 1 and No. 2 ranked teams in the nation. Weasler survived a 39-shot bombardment that night and backstopped a 3-2 win, before the two teams skated to a 2-2 tie back at the National Hockey Center the following night, with SCSU taking three of a possible four points on the weekend. When the next set of rankings came out, the Huskies again owned the No. 1 spot in the USCHO poll, and spent the next five weeks atop that perch.

They had lost only twice as the calendar rolled over to 2002, having dropped a Saturday matchup Dec. 8 in Colorado Springs against a CC team that included 2003 Hobey Baker winner Peter Sejna, Colin Stuart, Curtis McElhinney and Mark and Joe Cullen of Moorhead, younger brothers of former Huskies star Matt Cullen. But as the second half of the season progressed, the only conference sweeps SCSU managed came against Michigan Tech and Anchorage. Still, as the Huskies entered the final weekend of the regular season ranked second in the nation, and facing No. 4 Minnesota in the finalé for a third straight year, they had a chance to claim a share of the MacNaughton Cup. They trailed first-place Denver — who finished their slate with a series at North Dakota — by a single point. But this time, it was the Gophers playing their best hockey at the optimal time of year, and tables were turned — both in a home-and-away series sweep that weekend and in Minnesota's 4-1 win in the WCHA semifinal at the Xcel two weeks later.

For a seventh consecutive year though, the Huskies did make it to the WCHA Final Five, courtesy of a home sweep over Minnesota-Duluth in the first round. After falling to the Gophers in the semis though, they lost to Colorado College for the third time that season in the third-place game, and entered the 2002 NCAA tournament in a bit of a funk. The assignment they received was not a favorable one, again drawing the University of Michigan, and again having to travel to play the Wolverines on their own turf — this time to their home rink, Yost Arena in Ann Arbor, one of the most intimidating places to play in college hockey.

A unique wrinkle of the national tournament in 2002, coming only six months after the tragic attacks of 9/11, was the NCAA's decree that in an effort to minimize travel for as many teams as possible that for all championship tournaments that spring, any team within 400 miles of a regional site — Ann Arbor in the West and Worcester, Mass., in the East for men's hockey — would automatically be put in that regional and travel there by bus. That was a departure from previous years when the bottom two seeds from the east and west were swapped to mix things up a bit — which applied to this tournament theoretically would have sent the Huskies, seeded fifth, out east to face the No. 4 seed in that regional, Cornell, instead of facing the Wolverines in their home state for a second

MOUNT RUSHMORE
OF
HUSKY HOCKEY

VICE PRESIDENT WILLIAM RADOVICH

THE PIONEERS WHO TOOK THE PROGRAM TO DIVISION I
1987

PRESIDENT BRENDAN McDONALD

THE HOUSE THEY BUILT,
NATIONAL HOCKEY CENTER - 1989

JOHN MARIUCCI
"GODFATHER OF MINNESOTA HOCKEY"

HERB BROOKS
SCSU COACH

DR. MORRIS KURTZ
ATHLETIC DIRECTOR

CRAIG DAHL
ASST. COACH

straight year. That meant the West Regional in 2002 featured six of the top nine ranked teams in the nation, while the East featured all three of the lowest-ranked teams involved in the tournament. "People can complain about the criteria of travel based upon 9/11, but those of us from the East can sort of tell the sports fans to take off their microscopes and think about what's going on in the world. This is only sports," explained Jack McDonald, then-chairman of the NCAA Division I men's ice hockey tournament, and Quinnipiac's athletic director.

Unfortunately for St. Cloud State, while Worcester was very much a "neutral" site for all the six teams competing there — Boston University and Harvard were closest to the city, a little less than 45 miles, and no school was more than 300 miles away — there are few rinks in the country where a team enjoys a bigger home-ice advantage than the University of Michigan does at Yost Ice Arena. As *Michigan Daily* sports writer Michael Florek described a game at Yost in May 2010, "Games at Yost have turned into a non-stop tirade against the refs, the opposing team, its fans and, more importantly, its goalie. It starts before the first puck is dropped as fans tell referees to 'check the net!' and after the official has done so, to 'check it again!' The opposing player introductions are met with newspaper reading by the student section. ... With the volume, the intermission antics and the raucous multitude of mean-spirited chants comes the fact that these fans are some of the most knowledgeable college hockey fans in the country."

With that atmosphere as the backdrop to the Huskies' experience at the 2002 NCAA West Regional, the Wolverines scored three times on 11 shots in the first period before Weasler gave way to Moreland to begin the second. St. Cloud actually outshot Michigan in the second (and third), and neither side dented the net in the middle 20 minutes. Jon Cullen scored SCSU's second power-play goal of the night to cut the lead to 3-2 at the 4:19 mark of the last period, and in the moments that followed the Huskies came ever so close to drawing even in two excruciating near misses. About two minutes after Cullen's tally, Ryan Malone deposited the puck in the net for what appeared to be the tying goal. But that goal, like the score that clinched the Broadmoor at the WCHA Final Five a year earlier, went to video replay to see if an offensive player was in the crease when the puck went in. Replay showed that freshman Peter Szabo did not factor in the play at all and never interfered with goaltender Josh Blackburn, but he was in the crease when Malone scored, and the tying goal was waved off.

Moments later as the Huskies were busy killing a penalty, Hartigan picked off an extremely ill-conceived outlet pass from a Michigan defenseman, creating a long breakaway. The defenseman tried to wing the puck up ice to a Wolverine forward hanging out near the offensive blue line on the opposite side of the rink about 150 feet away. There's not another player on the team — on any team that year — the Huskies would rather have breaking in alone on the goaltender with a chance to tie an NCAA tournament game in the enemy's building. Hartigan, the nation's leading goal scorer that year with 37, skated in alone on Blackburn for what seemed like forever and wound up for a full-speed, point-blank left-handed slapshot from the middle of the circle on Blackburn's blocker side. The senior netminder fell into the butterfly just as Hartigan deked to his backhand, completely fooled and totally helpless to watch as Hartigan flipped the puck into an empty net for a 3-3 tie.

Except he didn't. As he skated around the prone Blackburn and reached to try to coral the puck, he couldn't quite get enough on the shot to put it in the yawning cage, and it slid about two inches wide. The score remained 3-2, and the Huskies were never able to get the equalizer. Dwight Helminen added a goal later in the third for the final margin, and the next night Michigan knocked off Denver, the WCHA regular season and playoff champs that year, for a return trip to the Frozen Four.

The Wolverines got a dose of their own medicine there, facing top-ranked Minnesota at the Xcel Energy Center in St. Paul two weeks later and falling in the semifinals. Minnesota topped the Maine Black Bears in overtime in the final for its first national championship since Herb Brooks roamed the bench in 1979. On the Friday between the semifinals and title game, Hartigan joined Gophers defenseman Jordan Leopold and New Hampshire sniper Darren Haydar in St. Paul as one of three "Hobey Hat Trick" finalists for college hockey's top honor. Minnesota's Leopold, the first Gophers defenseman ever to score 20 goals in a season, came away with the hardware, but Hartigan's own haul was still quite impressive.

In addition to single-season offensive records that still stand today, he was named St. Cloud State's first WCHA Player of the Year and its first NCAA First-Team All-American (West); he was an All-WCHA First-Team selection after being named to the Third Team the year prior; and he led the league with 24 goals and 49 points in 28 conference games. He gave up his final year of eligibility to sign with the Atlanta Thrashers and made his NHL debut on April 2 in Calgary. He left the program ranking third on the career points list with 165, behind only Jeff Saterdalen and Tim Hanus, and ranked fifth as the 2013-14 season got underway. His 86 career goals are still a record.

"I attribute my breakout that year to hard work in the summer months in Brainerd, where I believe my skating and foot speed really improved," Hartigan recalls. He saw action in 102 NHL games with the Thrashers, Columbus Blue Jackets (where Duvie Westcott was a teammate), Anaheim Ducks and Detroit Red Wings, and earned Stanley Cup rings in back-to-back seasons with the Ducks (2007, along with Joe Motzko) and Red Wings (2008).

While Hartigan was the headliner, several other Huskies were honored for their accomplishments as well: Nate DiCasmiro closed out his senior season with a nod to the All-WCHA Second Team and ended his career with 136 points, the ninth most among Huskies in the Division I era. And a trio of SCSU newcomers were named to the WCHA All-Rookie Team: forwards Mike Doyle and Peter Szabo, and defenseman Matt Gens.

The 2000-01 and 2001-02 seasons had been the two most successful campaigns in the history of SCSU men's hockey at that point, but with DiCasmirro's graduation and Hartigan's departure for an NHL contract with the Atlanta Thrashers that offseason, a great deal of the team's firepower needed replacing in seasons to come. Motzko led St. Cloud State with 42 points as a senior the next season, 2002-03, and the Huskies' best players that year were mostly upperclassmen: fellow seniors Jon Cullen (16 goals, 21 assists, 37 points); Ryan Malone (16 goals and 36 points in an injury-stunted 27-game season); and junior Matt Hendricks (a team-high 18 goals and 36 points). Senior Jake Moreland played the majority of the team's games in goal, but freshman Jason Montgomery saw action in 15 games.

That year's edition finished only a game above .500 — both overall and in league play — and was sixth in the WCHA and hit the road to Duluth for the first round of the WCHA playoffs, where it went the distance with the Bulldogs but lost in three games. In most seasons and most conferences, finishing sixth in the league and losing in the first round would be a death sentence for NCAA postseason hopes, but the tournament was expanded from 12 to 16 teams that year and the Huskies drew a No. 4 seed in the Northeast Regional in Worcester, Mass. There they faced off with top seed New Hampshire, ranked third in the nation and playing only 95 miles from its campus in Durham. The Wildcats' Colin Hemingway scored his first of two goals on the night only 10 seconds into the first period, and things didn't get much better from there. When the final horn sounded, New Hampshire had advanced with a 5-2 win and beat Hockey East rival Boston University, 3-0, the next night for a return trip to the Frozen Four, where they'd lost to Maine in St. Paul in 2002. The Wildcats made it all the way to the championship game before being overwhelmed by Minnesota in the final, the Gophers second straight NCAA championship. The loss to UNH marked the end of the line for Motzko and Malone, who finished their college days with 142 and 140 points, respectively, ranking fourth and fifth in school history at the time (they sat seventh and eighth entering 2013-14).

The team got off to a hot start in 2003-04, winning eight of its first nine games, highlighted by sweeps at home against Wisconsin and on the road at Minnesota-Duluth, and spent some time in the top 10 of the USCHO.com poll. But it wasn't long thereafter before things fell apart down the stretch and SCSU stumbled to another sixth-place finish. The Huskies finished the season with four straight losses to the Gophers at Mariucci— on March 5-6 to end the regular season, and the next weekend in the first round of the WCHA Playoffs. This time, there would be no reprieve when all the conference tournament action wrapped up, and the Huskies missed the NCAA tournament for the first time in five years. Matt Hendricks, the team's senior captain and a former state champion at Blaine High School as a senior in 2000, called it a career with 54 goals and 112 points on his NCAA resumé. A Predators fifth-round pick in 2000, he made his professional debut in one game of action with Nashville's AHL affiliate, the Milwaukee Admirals, and played most of the next five seasons in the minors before finally making his NHL debut with the Colorado Avalanche in 2008-09. Once there, he found a niche as a tough, hard-nosed grinding forward and became

SCSU Hockey
Joins
National Collegiate Hockey Conference

Colorado College
University of Denver
University of Miami (Ohio)
University of Minnesota-Duluth
University of North Dakota
University of Nebraska-Omaha
St. Cloud State University
Western Michigan University

NCHC Commisioner
Jim Scherr

Minneapolis Mayor
RT Rybak,

Target Center VP
Steve Mattson

est. 2013

SCSU Special Athletics Advisor
Gino Gasparini

SCSU President
Dr. Earl Potter III

a regular with the Washington Capitals before signing a four-year deal with the team that initially drafted him, the Predators, in the summer of 2013 — on the same day Matt Cullen inked a deal with Nashville.

Expecting to win (2005- 2009)

In 2004-05, a transfer from Providence College who had previously been Team USA's starting goaltender at the 2003 World Junior Championships practiced with the team all season, getting to know his new teammates as he sat out a required season as part of the NCAA's transfer rules: Bobby Goepfert. Those associated with the team had a hunch they had brought in a "difference maker" — he'd been the USHL Goaltender of the Year and Player of the Year with the Cedar Rapids RoughRiders in 2001-02 — but nobody could have predicted the kind of impact the Kings Park, N.Y., native ended up having. Goepfert was an NCAA West Second-Team All-American both his years with the Huskies — the team's only two-time All-American in Division I history — and that first season played more than even Brian Leitza in his record-setting senior year, equaling the SCSU legend's record with 38 games playing and topping him with 2,264 minutes played. His save totals in those seasons still stand as the second- and third-most in a season in school history.

St. Cloud State won only 14 games that year and only eight games in WCHA play, its fewest since going 8-16-4 in league games in 1998-99 — the only other time the Huskies had failed to reach double digits in victories. Dave Iannazzo, part of the all-freshman line that also included Mike Doyle and talented Slovakian Peter Szabo in 2001-02, led the team with 32 points in his final season. SCSU graduated four seniors that year — Iannazzo, Doyle, Szabo and defenseman Matt Gens, the team's captain. Seeded eight in the league playoffs that spring, the Huskies went to Colorado College and were swept, and that was that.

A little more than a month before the start of the 2005-06 season, Dahl stepped down as the team's head coach after 18 seasons — stunning the team and college hockey fans across the country — to pursue business opportunities in the private sector. Bob Motzko, an SCSU alum who played for John Perpich in the mid-1980s and was an assistant coach a year after graduating in Herb Brooks' one season on campus, took over the top job. Motzko was previously an assistant under Don Lucia at Minnesota for the previous four seasons, beginning with the Gophers' back-to-back national championship seasons, and had been hired over the summer to be Dahl's assistant. "I had a tremendous experience as a student athlete at SCSU. Some of my best friends are guys I played college hockey with. Since I decided to make a career out of coaching college hockey, one of my goals was to return to SCSU," said Motzko. He was named the interim head coach when Dahl announced he was leaving on Sept. 1, and the "interim" tag was lifted on Jan. 9, 2006. The team stood at 9-9-3 when his status was made official then went on a hot streak right after, splitting a series at Denver the following weekend before rattling off three consecutive sweeps in league play — over Minnesota-Duluth, at North Dakota and at home against Anchorage.

Joe Jensen, the Huskies' senior standout who went on to play with the Carolina Hurricanes in 2007-08 before continuing his career in Europe, had played under Motzko as a USHL rookie with the Sioux Falls Stampede in 2000-01. "Motzko had the same coaching style in college as he did in juniors. He gave his skilled players more freedom to make plays but expected a hard work ethic from everyone. To me, he had the most rounded skill set to motivate each type of player."

Still, after being swept at Wisconsin to end the regular season, the Huskies were .500 in conference games (13-13-2) and drew the sixth seed, heading to Colorado Springs for the second straight year for the first round of the WCHA playoffs. This time, however, SCSU sprung the upset, prevailing in three games and setting up a date with UMD in the play-in game at the Final Five the next weekend. That game proved to be a mismatch, as senior Billy Hengen scored 44 seconds into the first period, followed by goals from fellow senior Brock Hooton and sophomore Nate Dey — Minnesota's Mr. Hockey at North St. Paul High School in 2002-03, the first ever winner of that award to pull on a Huskies sweater. Sophomore Andrew Gordon — who led SCSU with 20 goals and 40 points in the regular season — scored in the third period and Hengen added his second goal for a very convincing 5-1 win. Goepfert kept busy making 36 saves to anchor the winning effort.

COACH'S CORNER

RALPH THEISEN
1931-32

LUDWIG ANDOLSEK
1932-35

ROBERT DEPAUL
1935-36

GEORGE LYNCH
1938-42

ROLAND VANDELL
1946-50 & 51-52

RAY GASPERLINE
1950-51

BRENDAN MCDONALD
1953-54

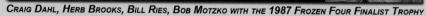

CRAIG DAHL, HERB BROOKS, BILL RIES, BOB MOTZKO WITH THE 1987 FROZEN FOUR FINALIST TROPHY

JIM BAXTER
1954-56

JACK WINK
1956-68

CHARLIE BASCH
1968-84

JOHN PERPICH
1984-86

HERB BROOKS
1986-87

CRAIG DAHL
1987-2005

BOB MOTZKO
2005-PRESENT

That set up a semifinal meeting on St. Patrick's Day with the nation's No. 1-ranked team, the Golden Gophers, on Saturday night at the Xcel Energy Center. That loaded Minnesota team featured a senior class that had won a national title as freshmen in 2003 (including St. Cloud Apollo grad Chris Harrington), as well as the most talented freshmen class in the country, led by future NHL stars Phil Kessel and Blake Wheeler. But the engine that made the team go was a pair of imports from North Dakota, Ryan Potulny and Danny Irmen; and sophomore defenseman Alex Goligoski. There really wasn't a weak spot in the lineup, and one might figure if the Huskies were to prevail, they'd need Goepfert to stand on his head.

Before the Huskies even left their hotel for the arena, the Xcel public address announcer had already anointed Minnesota the winner, proclaiming that North Dakota, 4-3 winners over eventual-national champions Wisconsin in the afternoon session, would play the Gophers in Saturday's championship. In front of the largest crowd to date in WCHA Final Five history, the two teams played even, 2-2, through the first period before the Huskies chased starter Kellen Briggs with a three-goal outburst in the first 6 minutes of the second to take a 5-2 advantage. Potulny got one back about midway through the period but Hooton answered less than 2 minutes later to restore the three-goal lead. And that's when things got a little crazy in St. Paul.

Potulny scored twice more to complete his hat trick before the final horn sounded to end the middle period, including a power-play marker making it 6-5 with the clock reading 0.4 seconds left before intermission. Things cooled down considerably for most of the final 20 minutes following that seven-goal scoring binge, which was just fine for SCSU's liking. Hooton took advantage of a Gophers turnover and scored unassisted with 3:39 left to give the Huskies a 7-5 lead, and it looked like the team would be playing for the Broadmoor Trophy again, for the first time since winning it in 2001.

Irmen scored with 2:01 left in regulation to again cut the lead to one — with Potulny earning an assist for his fourth point of the game. Minnesota had substituted freshman Jeff Frazee in Briggs' place in the second, but SCSU had stuck by their rock, Goepfert. With Frazee off for an extra skater as the final seconds ticked away, Potulny scored his fourth goal of the game with 15 seconds remaining for a stunning 7-7 tie. The partisan crowd at the Xcel went wild. No doubt many of the Gophers fans in attendance assumed it would be their team to score the winning goal when overtime began.

But once again, the Huskies weren't concerned what the script said was expected from them against the nation's top-ranked team. Fittingly, it was a St. Cloud native — 2003 Apollo grad Matt Hartman — that decided things, beating Frazee with a sharp-angle shot 9:14 into the extra session for an 8-7 SCSU win. "That was the most memorable and thrilling moment of my hockey career," Hartman said looking back at that game years later. "I was so happy for our loyal fans and for our team, which at the time was playing some of our best hockey we had played during my four years as a Husky. Beating the Gophers, who I've despised since childhood, in a packed Xcel Center with so many highs and lows will be something my teammates and I will remember forever."

The team played for the Broadmoor Final Five Championship the next day — once again facing the North Dakota Fighting Sioux, as it had in 2001 — and this time there was also an automatic NCAA tournament berth on the line as well. Knowing their resumé wasn't strong enough to earn a bid without a victory that night, there was some added pressure on the Huskies, but the team was buoyed with the memory of a sweep in Grand Forks the last weekend of January. Senior Konrad Reeder staked SCSU to an early lead with a power-play goal 3:50 into the first, but the Sioux answered with three goals of their own, including Rastislav Spirko tying things only 10 seconds after Reeder's tally. Future Stanley Cup captain and Conn Smythe Trophy winner Jonathan Toews also scored before the first intermission, as did T.J. Oshie, another future NHL standout, to extend UND's lead to 3-1. Ryan Duncan, the Hobey Baker Award winner the following year, scored a pair of goals in the second and by the time Hooton scored his fourth goal of the weekend and Hengen scored his third, it was all but a moot point as the team couldn't conquer goalie Jordan Parisé, losing 5-3.

It was St. Cloud's sixth game in nine days, including travel, as junior defenseman Casey Borer notes, and when it was decided the Huskies had little more than memories to share and stories to tell for their efforts. "Each guy knew what a huge milestone it would be for our program if we could win. Unfortunately, we came up short that night and it was a missed opportunity. That game still haunts me as the Final Five rolls into St. Paul each year," Borer said.

Team Records

Year	GM	W	L	T	Pct.	Coach
1931-32	8	1	7	0	.125	Ralph Theisen
1932-33	11	10	1	0	.909	Ludwig Andolsek
1933-34	9	7	1	1	.833	Ludwig Andolsek
1934-35	27	25	2	0	.926	Ludwig Andolsek
1935-36	11	6	5	0	.545	Robert DePaul
1936-37	10	5	5	0	.500	Walter Gerzin
1937-38	8	4	4	0	.500	Benedict Vandell
1938-39	9	5	4	0	.556	George Lynch
1939-40	11	6	5	0	.545	George Lynch
1940-41	10	4	4	2	.500	George Lynch
1941-42	7	5	2	0	.714	George Lynch
1942-46						WWII - No Teams
1946-47	19	14	3	2	.789	Roland Vandell
1947-48	16	12	4	0	.750	Roland Vandell
1948-49	12	6	6	0	.500	Roland Vandell
1949-50	13	7	6	0	.538	Roland Vandell
1950-51	8	5	3	0	.625	Ray Gasperline
1951-52	6	0	6	0	.000	Roland Vandell
1952-53	11	8	3	0	.727	George Martin
1953-54	4	2	2	0	.500	Brendan McDonald
1954-55	8	7	1	0	.875	Jim Baxter
1955-56	15	11	3	1	.767	Jim Baxter
1956-57	11	5	6	0	.455	Jack Wink
1957-58	9	4	5	0	.444	Jack Wink
1958-59	12	6	6	0	.500	Jack Wink
1959-60	13	11	2	0	.846	Jack Wink
1960-61	13	12	1	0	.923	Jack Wink
1961-62	12	12	0	0	1.000	Jack Wink
1962-63	7	5	1	1	.786	Jack Wink
1963-64	6	3	2	1	.583	Jack Wink
1964-65	9	5	4	0	.556	Jack Wink
1965-66	14	4	10	0	.286	Jack Wink
1966-67	15	1	14	0	.067	Jack Wink
1967-68	19	1	18	0	.053	Jack Wink
1968-69	20	2	18	0	.100	Charles Basch
1969-70	17	7	10	0	.412	Charles Basch
1970-71	17	10	7	0	.588	Charles Basch
1971-72	16	7	9	0	.438	Charles Basch
1972-73	20	8	12	0	.400	Charles Basch

Year	GM	W	L	T	Pct.	Coach
1973-74	23	15	6	2	.714	Charles Basch
1974-75	25	16	9	0	.640	Charles Basch
1975-76	24	9	14	1	.391	Charles Basch
1976-77	24	10	13	1	.435	Charles Basch
1977-78	24	12	12	0	.500	Charles Basch
1978-79	24	10	13	1	.435	Charles Basch
1979-80	30	20	9	1	.689	Charles Basch
1980-81	31	19	11	1	.633	Charles Basch
1981-82	29	14	15	0	.482	Charles Basch
1982-83	29	11	18	0	.379	Charles Basch
1983-84	28	11	17	0	.393	Charles Basch
1984-85	29	14	13	2	.519	John Perpich
1985-86	29	16	11	2	.593	John Perpich
1986-87	36	25	10	1	.714	Herb Brooks
1987-88	37	11	25	1	.327	Craig Dahl
1988-89	37	19	16	2	.514	Craig Dahl
1989-90	38	17	19	2	.447	Craig Dahl
1990-91	41	18	19	4	.466	Craig Dahl
1991-92	37	14	21	2	.378	Craig Dahl
1992-93	36	15	18	3	.417	Craig Dahl
1993-94	38	21	13	4	.553	Craig Dahl
1994-95	38	17	20	1	.447	Craig Dahl
1995-96	39	13	22	4	.333	Craig Dahl
1996-97	40	23	13	4	.575	Craig Dahl
1997-98	40	22	16	2	.550	Craig Dahl
1998-99	39	16	18	5	.410	Craig Dahl
1999-00	40	23	14	3	.575	Craig Dahl
2000-01	41	31	9	1	.768	Craig Dahl
2001-02	42	29	11	2	.714	Craig Dahl
2002-03	38	17	16	5	.513	Craig Dahl
2003-04	38	18	16	4	.526	Craig Dahl
2004-05	40	14	23	3	.388	Craig Dahl
2005-06	42	22	16	4	.571	Bob Motzko
2006-07	40	22	11	7	.638	Bob Motzko
2007-08	40	19	16	5	.538	Bob Motzko
2008-09	38	18	17	3	.513	Bob Motzko
2009-10	43	24	14	5	.616	Bob Motzko
2010-11	38	15	18	5	.461	Bob Motzko
2011-12	39	17	17	5	.500	Bob Motzko
2012-13	42	25	16	1	.609	Bob Motzko

Coach Ludwig Andolsek gives pointers to Goalie Arthur Salpacka

Coach Charlie Basch patrols the bench

Motzko, barely half a calendar year after taking over the program, was named the co-winner of the WCHA Coach of the Year award, sharing the honor with Minnesota's Don Lucia. The Gophers, meanwhile, were shut out by Wisconsin in the third-place game earlier that Saturday. When they took the ice again a week later, as the No. 1 seed in the West Regional in Grand Forks, they were knocked out of the tournament courtesy of a 4-3 overtime loss to Holy Cross, the unheralded champions of Atlantic Hockey, one of the most stunning upsets in the history of college hockey.

Led by Goepfert, an NCAA All-American and All-WCHA First Teamer for the second time each, St. Cloud State cruised to a second-place finish in Motzko's second year, 2006-07, equaling its best league finishes in school history in 2000-01 and '01-02. After three consecutive ties in early November, the Huskies strung together a 12-game win streak through Christmas and New Year's — and from Nov. 17 to Feb. 10, lost only twice. In addition to Goepfert's outstanding goaltending feats, a precocious tandem of freshman imports propelled SCSU back to the ranks of the WCHA elite. Andreas Nodl led the team with 46 points — the first freshman to lead the team in points since Matt Cullen in 1995-96 — and finished the season as the WCHA Rookie of the Year, the first in school history, as well as the NCAA Division I Rookie of the Year. Almost as good as Nodl, Lake Forest, Calif., native Ryan Lasch finished third on the club with 39 points, and like his Austrian classmate scored seven times on the power play. Another member of that class of newcomers was Garrett Raboin, whose 83 points when he graduated four years later ranked third in club history among defensemen since SCSU went Division I. Junior Andrew Gordon, who at season's end surrendered his final year of eligibility to sign with the Washington Capitals, led the Huskies with 22 goals (and 12 with a man advantage) and had only one point fewer than Nodl.

Entering the final weekend of the regular season, St. Cloud found itself two points behind the Gophers atop the league standings, but with a tough assignment — hosting North Dakota while Minnesota was at home against Michigan Tech. The Huskies skated to a hard-fought 3-3 tie against the Sioux, but the Gophers clinched the MacNaughton Cup with a 3-1 win over Tech, and it mattered not when both teams lost their Saturday rematches — though the Sioux, by virtue of their win at the National Hockey Center, giving them three out of a possible four points, leapfrogged Denver into third place.

The Huskies needed all three games (and then some) to get past a game Minnesota-Duluth squad in their first-round series after the Bulldogs came up with a 3-1 win in the Friday opener. And while three games in three nights is grueling enough, it ended up being more than four games worth of hockey by the time it was decided. Needing to win Saturday to force a third game, the Huskies led 2-1 late in the third when UMD tied it with 3:54 to play in regulation. Ryan Lasch had scored a power-play goal midway through the second that, at the time, gave SCSU a 2-0 lead, but on the night they were a miserable 1-for-9 on the power play, and that turned out to be the team's only success on 22 man-advantage opportunities in the series.

Nonetheless, Nate Dey finally finished the job 17 minutes into overtime, and the two teams began preparing for a decisive Game 3 on Sunday. Heading into the third period of that one, the Bulldogs had claimed a 2-1 lead with Lasch scoring St. Cloud's only goal with 1:27 to play in the opening period. Sophomore John Swanson, a St. Cloud Tech product, evened things at 2-2 with a goal 4:11 into the third period, and from there it was another 67 minutes, 22 seconds before another goal was scored by either team, when Nodl's shot from the left faceoff circle sent the Huskies on to St. Paul. It was the longest game ever for both programs, and the fifth-longest game in Division I men's ice hockey history. All told, the two teams played 248 minutes, 34 seconds of hockey on the weekend — more than four regulation games.

For senior Dan Kronick, the win was especially meaningful, as the former Holy Angels prep star had played his first two college seasons at UMD before transferring to St. Cloud. "The game was long, but losing never crossed my mind. It's hard to explain, but I felt we were going to win and it was just a matter of time before someone scored," Kronick said. "I was trying to catch my breath after a long shift, then Nodl scored and I instantly didn't feel tired anymore. I threw my gloves and stick in the air and one of my gloves hit Coach Motzko in the face. We all had a good laugh about that after we got back to the locker room."

The Final Five proved anticlimactic, and perhaps the team was still a little gassed after so much hockey the weekend before. Jonathan Toews, T.J. Oshie, Ryan Duncan and the rest of the formidable North Dakota lineup came out of the Xcel Center with a 6-2 semifinal win Friday. The following day the Huskies lost

Assistant Coaches Finding Future Huskies

Name	Year
AYERS, MIKE	2009-11
CARROLL, TODD	1990-91
CHRISTIAN, RYAN	1990-91
DAHL, CRAIG	1986-87
DELCASTILLO, DOC	1998-02
EAVES, MIKE	1987-88
FRANTTI, BILL	1994-03
GALBRATH, DAN	1992-93
GIBBONS, MIKE	2007-PRESENT
HARBINSON, FRED	2002-07
HARRINGTON, JOHN	1990-93
HASTINGS, MIKE	1988-92, 93-94
JOHNSON, JUSTIN	2006-09
JOHSNON, STEVE	2010-12
LANGEVIN, DAVE	1990-91
MORINVILLE, DAVE	1988-90
MOTZKO, BOB	1986-87
NORGEN, MARK	1987-88
PETERSEN, BRETT	1994-00
RABOIN, GARRETT	2012-PRESENT
RIES, BILL	1986-87
ROGALSKI, DAVE	2011-PRESENT
RUD, ERIC	2005-10
SERRATORE, TOM	1993-99
STRELOW, RICK	1991-92
WENINGER, DAVID	2004-05
WILNER, BRAD	2000-05

ERIC RUD

BRETT PETERSEN

FRED HARBINSON

TOM SERRATORE

MIKE HASTINGS

MIKE GIBBONS

BILL FRANTTI

STEVE JOHNSON

GARRETT RABOIN

DOC DELCASTILLO

FUTURE ASSISTANT JOHN HARRINGTON
ASSISTS ON GAME WINNER MIRACLE GOAL

FORMER NORTH STAR
MIKE EAVES

in overtime, 4-3, to Wisconsin in the third-place game, while the Sioux lost the title game, also in OT, to the top-seeded Gophers when Blake Wheeler's swat at the puck as he fell to the ice somehow found a tiny hole over Philippe Lamoureux's shoulder for the game-winner.

The Huskies watched the NCAA selection show the next day knowing they were comfortably in the field of 16, ending up with the No. 2 seed in the East Regional and a date with third seed Maine in Rochester, N.Y. But in what was becoming an all-too-familiar ending, and starting to become an all-too familiar talking point among NCAA hockey pundits, SCSU went "One and Done" at the national tournament. The Black Bears were led that day by future NHLers Teddy Purcell, with three assists, and goaltender Ben Bishop, who stopped 33 of 34 shots and slammed the door after Justin Fletcher's goal gave SCSU a 1-0 lead 3:39 into the opening period of a 4-1 win. Goepfert, meanwhile, finished off his superb career with 17 saves on 21 shots.

It turned out to be an opportunity squandered, as opposite them in the East bracket the No. 1 seed, Clarkson, was upset by UMass-Amherst. Future Conn Smythe Trophy winner with the Kings, Jonathan Quick, posted a 1-0 shutout for the Minutemen, making their first ever NCAA appearance. They could repeat the feat and get past Maine the next day and two weeks later the Black Bears were knocked off by Michigan State, which went on to win the national championship. Motzko was again named a co-winner of the WCHA Coach of the Year award, this time sharing with Michigan Tech's Jamie Russell. Both Goepfert and Gordon were named to the All-WCHA First Team, and Goepfert was one of 10 finalists for the Hobey Baker Award. While the Huskies still hadn't gotten "over the hump" in winning their first NCAA tournament game in school history, it was the start of a stretch of four NCAA appearances in seven seasons.

The Huskies were one of the youngest teams in the conference in 2007-08, but also one of its most talented as it boasted five NHL draft picks from its freshman class. This team would be major threats to its opponents as it returned a majority of its core players including the battle-tested captain Matt Stephenson. As good as Ryan Lasch was as a freshman, he was even better as a sophomore, leading the WCHA with 34 points in league play (17 goals, 17 assists), and with 53 overall, fifth most in the country, earning a spot on the All-WCHA First Team and as a Second-Team All-American. A Hobey Baker finalist at season's end, Lasch found instant chemistry with All-WCHA Rookie Team member Garrett Roe, who led all league newcomers with 28 points in conference games. Both Roe and Nodl were named to the All-WCHA Second Team, and all three finished in the top six in points — Lasch was second in goals in league play, Nodl had 15. Meanwhile Garrett Raboin, another sophomore, was one of the team's leading point producers from the blue line and Jase Weslosky, a second-year player who'd played in only six games as a freshman, won 16 games and appeared in 34 as a sophomore.

Tied for fourth in the league but receiving the fifth seed in the WCHA playoffs, St. Cloud hosted sixth seed Wisconsin in the first round. Weslosky saw 24 shots and stopped all of them in a Game 1 victory, with John Swanson, Lasch and Nodl providing the offense. The Badgers proved a tough out in the Saturday rematch for Game 2, outshooting their hosts by a wide margin, 49-21, and leading by a goal for a while in the second, but they could never pull away. It went to overtime and Lasch didn't make the folks wait too late, ending the Badgers' season with a goal 3:57 into the sudden death period. That earned a spot in the play-in game for the Huskies, opposite Minnesota.

Minnesota played its fourth game in seven days (fifth if one considers the overtimes against Mankato) and earned a dramatic win over the Huskies. Tony Lucia, the double-OT hero of Game 3 against the Mavs the weekend prior, traded goals in the first period with Raboin, and Evan Kaufman gave the Gophers a 2-1 lead heading into the third. That score held for much of the third until Tony Mosey tied it with 4:26 left, and the game seemed destined for overtime. But before it got their, St. Cloud Apollo grad Mike Howe flipped home a rebound with only 13 seconds left to send the Huskies home from the party early.

The Huskies had also done more than enough to secure a bid, and again drew the No. 2 seed in the East Regional, in a familiar location, Albany, N.Y., in the same arena where they faced Boston University in 2000. This time they got Clarkson, the ECAC regular season champions who had been knocked off in the first round of that league's playoffs by No. 8 seed Colgate. Neither team scored in the first period, and the Golden Knights dramatically outshot SCSU in the second, by a 14-5 margin, but both teams scored once and the score was 1-1 going into the final 20 minutes of regulation. Shea Guthrie scored the only goal of the third, with an assist from future NHL defenseman Grant Clitsome, and Clarkson advanced with a 2-1 victory. For the second consecutive year — and the third

Minnesota High School Icons

Nate Dey - *North St. Paul HS*
Mr. Hockey 2003

Joey Benik - *St. Francis HS*
MSHSL Record - 65 Goals

Ben Hanowski - *Little Falls HS*
MSHSL Record - 405 Career points

Junior Hockey Legends

Nate DiCasmirro - *North Iowa*
USA Hockey Player of the Year 1998

Charlie Lindgren - *Sioux Falls*
USA Goalie of the Year 2013

Michael Olson - *Nanaimo*
Canadian Jr. Player of the Year 2005

time in program history — the Huskies played as the higher seed (and thus the presumed favorite) in a first-round NCAA tournament game and came up empty, and the program's all-time NCAA tournament record stood at zero wins and eight losses. "I was devastated when we lost (to Clarkson), but at the same time I was encouraged because I knew the program was headed in the right direction," said junior defenseman David Carlisle. "I knew we would win some big games in the near future."

A few days after Clarkson eliminated St. Cloud, Andreas Nodl — the Flyers' 39th overall pick in 2006 — signed a professional contract and finished the 2007-08 season playing for the AHL's Philadelphia Phantoms. In the years since Nodl played 183 NHL games with Philly and the Carolina Hurricanes before heading home to Austria to play in his native country's top league in 2013-14. While the returning Huskies had plenty of individual success on the ice in 2008-09, the team stumbled to a .500 record in WCHA play. Ryan Lasch and Garrett Roe finished fourth and fifth, respectively, in points accumulated in league play, and Garrett Raboin was third on the team with both 10 goals and 33 points from the blue line overall. All three earned All-WCHA consideration, with Lasch getting a spot on the First Team.

Breakthrough (2009-present)

Few places in the world can rival southern California for its prolific production of fruits and vegetables — chances are you've eaten something originally grown there in the past week. But as hockey is concerned, it doesn't provide the most fertile soil for growing and developing future stars. The fact that any players with name recognition come from that part of the country is a very recent development, the result of a generation of kids deciding to lace up the ice (or in-line) skates and emulate Los Angeles Kings legends Wayne Gretzky and Luc Robitaille, or more recently Mighty Ducks of Anaheim luminaries Teemu Selanne and Paul Kariya.

St. Cloud State had never brought in a recruit in the Division I era that listed California as his home state until Ryan Lasch came to campus as a freshman in 2006. And even then, Lasch left home and headed way north to develop his game in Ontario, a more traditional growing environment for hockey, playing with the Pembroke Lumber Kings in Canadian Junior 'A' hockey before pulling on a Huskies sweater. He was born and raised in Lake Forest, Calif., in southern Orange County, about 20 miles from the Anaheim Ducks' home rink, and spent his youth at nearby Trabuco Hills High School. But unfortunately for Lasch and other talented athletes in that area with aspirations of playing hockey at a high level, options close to home are limited and the competition isn't as good as it is in northern climates (at least not yet).

The fact he stood only 5-foot-8 didn't help much, and given those two factors Lasch probably wasn't much known to hockey heads in the Central Canada Junior Hockey League when he headed for Pembroke, but that didn't last very long. He had 64 points as a rookie in 2004-05, and piled up an astonishing 68 goals and 146 points (both league bests by a wide margin) in only 56 games the following year, when he was named CJHL Player of the Year and committed to SCSU. His opponents in those two seasons included a pair of current Flyers standouts, Claude Giroux and Wayne Simmonds.

Having accumulated 134 points in his first three seasons at St. Cloud State, Lasch returned for his senior year already with more points than all but seven Huskies that came before him in the program's Division I history, and all but 11 total all-time. He was the first SCSU player named to the All-WCHA First Team twice and as a junior became the third player in school history named a Hobey Baker Award finalist. Only 45 points shy of Jeff Saterdalen's 18-year-old record for most career points, the prospect of a new No. 1 was a very real possibility — but it would take another great season from Lasch to get there. A lot has to go right to put together a year like that, including good health and help from teammates around you to make it happen.

A pair of youngsters from just up Highway 10 about 30 miles, who rewrote the Minnesota high school hockey record books in their prep days, would be key to the Huskies' fortunes that year and for several more to come. The numbers Jared Festler and Ben Hanowski produced at Little Falls seem almost impossible, like statistics out of a video game — it's almost tough not to get a little lost in them. Playing together in 2006-07 on a unit that also included Ben's older brother Beau, like Festler a junior that season, the Flyers' top line piled up 186 goals and 322 points. Festler, who later bypassed his senior year to play

2013 MacNaughton Cup Winners

junior hockey with the USHL's Lincoln Stars, scored 71 of those 186, a new Minnesota State High School League record that would last only two years, until Ben Hanowski scored 73 as a senior. Ben's 71 assists that final year with Festler as a linemate are the fourth most in MSHSL history, and as a senior in 2008-09 he racked up 135 points in only 31 games (an average of 4.35 per contest), breaking the 30-year old record of 131 set by Roseau's Aaron Broten in 1978-79. He also smashed Johnny Pohl's career points record, passing the former Red Wing and Gophers star's mark of 378 in late February just before section tournaments started. By the time he was done he had 405 (196 goals, 209 assists), an average of just more than 100 per season over four years. Included in that career total were 29 shorthanded goals. The Flyers played in the Class A state tournament for the fifth consecutive year in 2009, finally losing their first game of the season in the semifinals to Breck, who won the championship the next afternoon after the Flyers beat St. Cloud Cathedral for third place.

As a sophomore with SCSU in 2009-10, Festler was fifth on the team with 24 points, including a pair of goals in a 4-1 win at Minnesota on Jan. 23 that helped the Huskies secure a home-and-home sweep of the Gophers. Going straight from Little Falls High School to St. Cloud State, Hanowski had a fine rookie year and finished with nine goals and 19 points. With Jase Weslosky gone to graduation, St. Cloud turned to a rotation of junior Dan Dunn and a highly-touted recruit from Roseau, Mike Lee, who backstopped the Rams to the Class AA state championship as a sophomore in 2006-07. In the middle of his rookie season with the Huskies, Lee left the team to play for Team USA at the World Junior Championships in Saskatchewan. He helped the Americans win gold medals for only the second time in the history of the Under-20 event - the first since a Zach Parisé -led team won it in 2004- and in the process snapped the host Canadians' string of five consecutive first-place finishes at the tournament.

Lasch's campaign didn't get off to a fantastic start, and neither did St. Cloud's. He went without a point in a pair of losses at Miami (Ohio) to start 2009-10, and SCSU didn't pick up its first sweep until going to Anchorage and returning home with two wins the first weekend of December. Still, as the season progressed the California kid continued checking off a who's-who list of SCSU hockey alums as he passed them: Arnason, DiCasmirro, Passolt, Reichel, Malone, Motzko, Bergo, Brodzinski. Lasch put together an eight-game points streak from Nov. 13 to Dec. 5, chalking up seven goals and 11 points total, moving up from eighth all-time in school history to fourth, with only Mark Hartigan, Tim Hanus and Saterdalen still in front of him, though still with a way to go to catch them.

St. Cloud won nine games in a row to start the 2010 side of the calendar, including a three-assist performance from Lasch in a 5-1 nonconference win over visiting Brown on Jan. 2. He scored a goal and assisted on two others in a 6-0 blowout of Alaska-Anchorage at the National Hockey Center on Feb. 5 to tie and then pass Hartigan, finishing the evening with 167 points. He set up two goals at Wisconsin on Feb. 20 for his 172nd and 173rd career points, equaling and passing Hanus, but the Huskies fell, 7-4, to the Badgers at the Kohl Center.

The Huskies finished 15-9-4 and in third place in the WCHA, and hosted a familiar foe in the first round of the playoffs. St. Cloud may have been the home team and the favorite, but they'd just finished the regular season with a home-and-home with Minnesota State-Mankato in which they managed just one of a possible four points, limping to the finish line. They'd need all three games that weekend to finally eliminate the Mavericks.

They led 3-0 a little more than halfway through Game 1 before losing in overtime, with Kael Mouillierat scoring the game-winner only 20 seconds into the extra session. It looked for all the world as though MSU might spring the upset for much of Saturday, and SCSU trailed 2-0 heading into the third. But freshman David Eddy scored 52 seconds into the final period and Garrett Roe scored a pair 20 seconds apart a few moments later for a 3-2 win. In the decisive Game 3 on Sunday, Roe and Garrett Raboin (the Huskies' captain for the second straight year) both scored for SCSU, but once again the game needed overtime to decide which team advanced. This time, sophomore Drew LeBlanc was the hero, scoring the winner 3:21 into sudden death. Lasch picked up two assists, including one on LeBlanc's OT tally, and moved within one point of Saterdalen on the all-time list.

Second-seeded Wisconsin was waiting for the Huskies in the first semifinal at the WCHA Final Five the following weekend. As it turned out, the Badgers went on to lose the national championship game a couple weeks later, losing to Boston College 5-0 at Ford Field in Detroit, home of the Lions. SCSU played the boys from Madison six times that season, and definitely held its own. The two teams split two earlier series — Nov. 20-21 in St. Cloud and Feb. 19-20 in the

POUND

WE ARE THE CHAMPIONS SC

GO HUSKIES!

2001 WCHA FINAL FIVE CHAMPIONS

Wisconsin capital. They'd split another pair of postseason games as well. It was the Huskies winning the first meeting in that semifinal, with Mike Lee stopping all 37 shots and Lasch and Travis Novak providing all the support he would need for a 2-0 win.

For the fourth time in school history, St. Cloud State played for the Broadmoor Trophy in the WCHA Final Five championship game — and for the third time, they met the University of North Dakota. Unlike their previous three bids for the league playoff title, the Huskies suited up in the home whites. It took only 40 seconds for Lasch to pick up career point No. 180, feeding Raboin with a centering pass after the defenseman ventured in from the point to join the attack and give SCSU a 1-0 lead. With that, he also passed Saterdalen, who was in attendance and visited with Lasch after the game, into first place on the school's all-time assists list. Fifteen seconds after Raboin's goal, Eddy scored and the Huskies had a 2-0 lead even before a full minute had ticked off the game clock. Corban Knight and Brad Malone answered to tie the game 2-2 before the first intermission. UND's Danny Kristo and Chris VandeVelde would score goals on the power play in the second to stake the Sioux to a lead they never relinquished on the way to a 5-3 win.

A return trip down Interstate 94 to St. Paul was booked for the following weekend after the Huskies got the No. 2 seed in the West Regional at the Xcel Energy Center — the first time an SCSU team had played an NCAA tournament game in their own Central time zone. There they got No. 3 seed Northern Michigan, an old acquaintance from the bygone days of an earlier WCHA. For Lasch and most of his senior teammates, it was their third NCAA tournament trip in four years.

And for the program, after eight previous tries and 23 years of waiting and hoping for a breakthrough at the NCAA Division I men's ice hockey tournament... the Huskies and their supporters were forced to wait a little more to find out if the program could finally put a notch in the 'W' column. SCSU twice led by two goals, at 2-0 and 3-1, but the Wildcats clawed back to even and the Huskies needed 20 minutes and an extra 23 seconds of overtime to finally celebrate an NCAA winner.

St. Cloud blitzed NMU to start the game, outshooting the Wildcats 17-6 in the first period and building a 2-1 lead. Both Lasch and Roe had power-play goals in the first 40 minutes of regulation, the latter of which made for a 3-1 lead after Travis Novak opened the scoring with a marker 8:14 into the game. Ray Kaunisto cut NMU's deficit to 3-2 with a goal 3:48 before the second intermission and that's where it stood when the horn sounded. Northern Michigan outshot SCSU 27-14 in the final two periods but Lee was typically up to the task, and as the clock ticked down with the Huskies still leading, fans, players and coaches alike probably couldn't help but steal a glance toward the clock a time or two. But with 3:49 left on the clock in regulation, the Wildcats scored, Erik Spady — his first goal of the season. Unbelievable. For those inclined to superstition, to believe in curses, this was ripe for doubt.

After the intermission though, St. Cloud got the better of chances in the first overtime, harassing Northern goaltender Brian Stewart with 22 shots in that frame. Finally Tony Mosey, a junior who played his prep hockey at Shattuck-St. Mary's in Faribault, redirected a pass from Roe past Stewart and into the net to end it. "It's a huge monkey off our back," said Mosey at the press conference afterward. With his power-play goal in the first, Lasch passed Saterdalen on the school's career goals list and finished with 79, behind only Mark Hartigan. Roe had three points, assisting on Lasch's score and Mosey's game-winner in addition to his power-play tally.

Opposite SCSU at the West Regional, top-seeded Wisconsin got through its first-round matchup against Vermont with a 3-2 win. The Madison squad that St. Cloud met in the regional final was laden with future NHL talent, much of it of the high-end variety: nine players from that group of Badgers had made NHL debuts heading into the 2013-14 season, and Derek Stepan, Ryan McDonagh, Craig Smith, Jake Gardiner and Justin Schultz were key regulars for their respective teams. Another, Blake Geoffrion, a fourth-generation NHLer, was a Predators second-round pick in 2006 and after a trade to Montreal was one of the Canadiens' top prospects before a scary injury forced him into retirement. In 2009-10, he led the WCHA with 19 goals and was second with 34 points in league play, one point behind leader Rhett Rakhshani of Denver. Five of UW's defensemen in that game went on to play in the NHL, and the sixth — John Ramage, the son of

WCHA FINAL FIVE 2006 EXCEL CENTER ST. PAUL, MN

HUSKIES BEAT THE GOPHERS 8-7 IN A THRILLING OVERTIME GAME VIEWED BY A RECORD-BREAKING STANDING ROOM ONLY CROWD OF 19,353

former blueliner Rob Ramage, a veteran of more than 1,000 NHL games — went on to wear the captain's 'C' for the Badgers each of his last two years and made his pro debut with the AHL's Abbotsford Heat in 2013-14.

Sophomore Jared Festler scored twice to highlight the Huskies effort that day, including a shorthanded tally in the early moments of the third period that at the time cut the Huskies' deficit to 3-2 and gave some hope. But St. Cloud State was doomed by it inability to convert on seven power-play opportunities. Mike Lee, who made 42 saves in the win over NMU, yielded three goals on 11 shots before giving way to Dan Dunn following Gardiner's goal making it 3-1 with 4:39 left in the first period. Mosey, the double-overtime hero of SCSU's first NCAA tournament win, scored the final goal of the season for the Huskies cutting the lead to 4-3 with 2:50 left in regulation before Wisconsin added an empty-netter. Coach Bob Motzko admitted in the press conference afterward that his team was a little drained after needing the extra time Friday to dispatch Northern Michigan. "The first period was a struggle for us. And we felt it on the bench. Our tanks were down. You're trying to encourage but you've got to fight through those moments." After the game was over, it took the emotional players over 60 minutes to get out of their gear. "It was heartbreaking to come so far and be so close to the first Frozen Four in school history," recalls forward Aaron Marvin. "Winning the first NCAA game wasn't the only legacy we wanted to leave behind that season, we felt we deserved more."

Lasch had three points in his final weekend of college hockey, and finished his career with 79 goals, 104 assists and 183 points, four more than Jeff Saterdalen. He ended up second in school history with 37 power-play goals, three short of Saterdalen's school record of 40, and was named to the All-WCHA Second Team after earning nods to the First Team the previous two years. "There have been so many unbelievable players that went to SCSU, I'm grateful for being provided the opportunity to achieve something so big," Lasch said of breaking the points record. "The individual success wouldn't have been possible without being surrounded by winning teams and outstanding guys."

Lasch and Roe, named to the Third Team, joined former star defenseman Kelly Hultgren as the only Huskies ever named all-conference three times. Raboin closed out his career with a nod to the Third Team as well, his second time as an all-conference performer. Garrett Roe, meanwhile, was named to the West Regional All-Tournament team, courtesy of his three-point game against the Wildcats. As he entered his senior year his career point total stood at 142, only one fewer than Lasch had through three seasons. For a second straight winter, it looked like SCSU fans would be watching a record chase.

Like Lasch, Roe came to St. Cloud State from a place not known for churning out hockey talent. To date, only four players in NHL history claim the state of Virginia as their place of birth. Roe came from a hockey family in Vienna, Va., and while he was also a very good soccer and lacrosse player, he was always partial to hockey. "Hockey's always been my No. 1 and I can't see it changing to something else," he told *Fairfax Times* reporter Reed S. Albers for a 2011 feature story near the end of his final NCAA season. He grew up playing for local youth teams, including the Washington Little Caps, but left Virginia at 14 to further his hockey career and pursue an NCAA scholarship. His first stop was Shattuck-St. Mary's in Faribault, then he played three years in the USHL with the Indiana Ice before coming to St. Cloud.

While Roe had another highly successful season in his SCSU finalé, he came up short of his old teammate's new points record. But when the Huskies season came to an the end following a triple-overtime loss at Minnesota-Duluth in the first round of the WCHA playoffs, Roe was the program's new career assists leader. He caught and passed Saterdalen in a home series against Michigan Tech on Jan. 7-8, and two weeks later passed Lasch with an assist on Jared Festler's goal in a 3-3 tie against Mankato at the National Hockey Center on Jan. 28.

The WCHA added two new teams in 2010-11, admitting Bemidji State and Nebraska-Omaha and increasing membership to 12. It proved to be a short-lived arrangement though, as Minnesota and Wisconsin announced on March 22, 2011, that they were leaving the WCHA to be founding members of the new Big Ten hockey conference following the 2012-13 NCAA season. With Penn State adding hockey as a varsity sport, the Big Ten now had six schools with men's hockey programs, and Michigan, Michigan State and Ohio State likewise abandoned the CCHA, causing massive upheaval in the college hockey landscape. When the dust settled, St. Cloud State ended up part of the new National Collegiate Hockey Conference, along with Minnesota-Duluth, North Dakota, Denver, Colorado

HUSKIES TOPPLE GOPHERS, OFF TO PLAY UND FOR CHAMPIONSHIP

2001 BROADMOOR TROPHY WINNERS

MATT HARTMAN, HOMETOWN HERO, NETS OT GAME WINNER AGAINST THE GOPHERS AND CELEBRATES WITH CAPTAIN CASEY BORER.

2012 HANDSHAKE LINE

NATE RADUNS AND JOHN SWANSON GOING HARD TO THE NET

2010 SCSU SQUAD DOWNS THE WISCONSIN BADGERS

MORRIS KURTZ PRESENTS TONY MOSEY WITH 2010 ALL-TOURNEY TEAM AWARD

BROCK HOOTON 2006 ALL-TOURNEY AWARD

TYLER ARNASON IS PRESENTED THE 2001 FINAL FIVE MVP

JOE JENSEN BURIES THE PUCK AGAINST THE GOPHERS

College and Nebraska-Omaha from the now lame-duck WCHA; and Miami (Ohio) and Western Michigan from the CCHA, which would cease to exist. That rendered the 2010-11 season and the two following it as the final trips through the WCHA for the Huskies.

St. Cloud stumbled to an eighth-place finish in the new 12-team league. Roe finished second on the team with 36 points that year, while junior Drew LeBlanc led the Huskies with 39 and tied for the team lead with 13 goals. The UMD squad that eliminated the Huskies, led by Hobey Baker finalist Jack Connolly, went on to win the first NCAA championship in Bulldogs history with an overtime win over Michigan in the final about a month later at the Xcel Energy Center, with North Dakota also representing the WCHA at the Frozen Four.

After leading the Huskies in points as a junior, it only made sense that Drew LeBlanc, already a two-time member of the WCHA All-Academic Team, would wear the captain's 'C' on his sweater for his final season of college hockey. After leading Hermantown High School to an undefeated season and a Class A state championship as a senior with the Hawks in 2007, LeBlanc had piled up 85 points in three seasons at St. Cloud State and seemed a cinch to join the program's "Century Club" as a college senior. He was off to a great start with 10 assists and 12 points through nine games when suddenly everything went horribly wrong.

The Huskies had whipped Wisconsin, 7-2, at the National Hockey Center on Nov. 4, 2011, and were going for a sweep in the Saturday rematch. Late in the second period, with his team leading 2-1, LeBlanc skated hard on a forecheck after a loose puck in the Badgers' end of the ice. Going pretty much full speed near the boards when he hit the brakes, he caught an edge and fell awkwardly, slammed violently into the boards and broke both bones in his lower leg, suffering a gruesome compound fracture. One didn't need a medical degree to realize the injury was going to end his season — and thus his college career. It was bad enough to wonder if he'd ever play competitive hockey again.

Two weeks prior to that, starting goaltender Mike Lee, another of SCSU's three captains along with fellow junior Ben Hanowski, suffered a leg injury in practice on the Monday following a nonconference series with New Hampshire. It was originally feared Lee would miss the rest of the season, and while he did return in late January, for now the Huskies faced a future without its best offensive player and top goaltender. Freshman Ryan Faragher filled in admirably in Lee's absence — and more importantly logged a ton of invaluable experience that would serve him well the following year — and while the team was much improved down the stretch in 2011-12, they managed only a sixth-place finish and ultimately missed the NCAA tournament for a second straight year.

Faragher was not your typical freshman — he was actually three months older than Lee and honed his game with the North American Hockey League's Bismarck Bobcats, winning a Robertson Cup playoff championship in 2010. And when Lee signed after his junior year with the Phoenix Coyotes, who drafted him in the third round in 2009, Faragher took over as the unquestioned starter as a sophomore for the first Frozen Four club in Huskies history in 2012-13.

SCSU had a first-round date with Nebraska-Omaha in the first round of the WCHA playoffs in a matchup of the No. 6 and 7 seeds, and faced little challenge in sweeping the Mavericks. After a 4-0 win on Friday, Saturday's Game 2 was tied at a goal apiece before Hanowski and fellow senior Travis Novak both scored in the final minute of regulation for a 3-1 clincher — the latter scoring an empty-net tally with less than a second remaining. Having reclaimed the starter's job by then, Lee stopped 59 of 60 shots he faced on the weekend for the wins. He was in net the following weekend for a play-in game against North Dakota at the Final Five, but St. Cloud fell 4-1 — with UND (no longer the "Fighting Sioux") scoring two empty-net goals in the final minute, as the Huskies tried desperately to tie the game and extend their season. Four WCHA teams made the NCAA tournament that spring, with the Gophers advancing to the Frozen Four in Tampa Bay, but the Huskies were left home.

There was plenty to be excited for at the start of the Huskies' last season in the WCHA, even if a preseason poll of league media picked them to finish sixth. Drew LeBlanc's broken leg had healed and he had petitioned the NCAA for, and received, a medical redshirt granting him a fifth year of eligibility and a do-over on his senior year. Once again he shared captains' duties with Ben Hanowski, SCSU's leader in goals (23) and points (43) the year before, and now a senior himself. Also back was a talented and deep group of defensemen led by Nick Jensen, a Red Wings draft pick named to the All-WCHA Third Team as a sophomore

NCAA FROZEN FOUR 1987

NCAA TOURNAMENT

YEAR	REGION	SITE	OPPONENT	ROUND	SCORE
1987	EAST	SALEM, MA	SALEM STATE VIKINGS	QUARTERFINALS	3-2 W (OT)
			SALEM STATE VIKINGS	QUARTERFINALS	2-1 W
	FROZEN 4	PLATTSBURGH, NY	OSWEGO STATE LAKERS	SEMIFINAL	2-5 L
		PLATTSBURGH, NY	BEMIDJI STATE BEAVERS	CONSOLATION	6-4 W
1989	EAST	SAULT STE. MARIE, MI	LAKE SUPERIOR ST LAKERS	FIRST	3-6 L
			LAKE SUPERIOR ST LAKERS	FIRST	2-4 L
2000	EAST	ALBANY, NY	BOSTON UNIV TERRIERS	FIRST	3-5 L
2001	WEST	GRAND RAPIDS, MI	MICHIGAN WOLVERINES	QUARTERFINALS	3-4 L
2002	WEST	ANN ARBOR, MI	MICHIGAN WOLVERINES	FIRST	2-4 L
2003	NE	WORCESTER, MA	NEW HAMPSHIRE WILDCATS	FIRST	2-5 L
2007	EAST	ROCHESTER, NY	MAINE BLACK BEARS	FIRST	1-4 L
2008	EAST	ALBANY, NY	CLARKSON GOLDEN KNIGHTS	FIRST	1-2 L
2010	WEST	ST. PAUL, MN	NORTHERN MICH WILDCATS	FIRST	4-3 W (2 OT)
			WISCONSIN BADGERS	QUARTERFINALS	3-5 L
2013	MIDWEST	TOLEDO, OH	NOTRE DAME FIGHTING IRISH	FIRST	5-1 W
			MIAMI RED HAWKS	QUARTERFINALS	4-1 W
	FROZEN 4	PITTSBURGH, PA	QUINNIPIAC BOBCATS	SEMIFINAL	1-4 L

the year before whose 32 points in 2011-12 ranked second among returning letterwinners; and Andrew Prochno, an All-WCHA Rookie Team honoree who chipped in 24 assists and 29 points as a freshman.

Joining the effort was a fine freshman class highlighted by Jonny Brodzinski, son of former SCSU star Mike Brodzinski who played for the Huskies their last three years of Division III. After playing in two Class AA state tournaments with Blaine, Jonny Brodzinski scored a team-high 22 goals as a freshman for St. Cloud in 2012-13, the most ever by a true freshman in school history. Joey Benik had 65 goals at St. Francis in 2008-09, the third most in a single season in the history of Minnesota prep hockey, behind only Ben Hanowski and Jared Festler. He wrapped up his high school career with the Saints with 283 career points in 2010 and joined the Huskies after two seasons with the Penticton Vees of the British Columbia Junior Hockey League. Kalle Kossila, the first player from Finland to play for SCSU, ended his first NCAA season tied for third on the team with Brodzinski with 33 points. Ethan Prow, a defenseman from nearby Sauk Rapids, chipped in 15 points from the blue line in his SCSU debut season.

The Huskies opened their last WCHA schedule with a home sweep of Minnesota State with identical 5-1 scores, with LeBlanc scoring a goal and assisting on three others in Friday's opener. For the next five series in conference play, SCSU earned splits each weekend before really starting to heat up as the calendar flipped to 2013. They swept Colorado College at the National Hockey Center in the final series before Winter Break, then won both games with Denver at home on Jan. 18-19 after a pair of nonconference series with RPI and Northern Michigan on either side of New Year's.

After coming home from North Dakota having taken three out of four points in Grand Forks the last weekend of January, the Huskies crept to No. 12 in the USCHO poll and jumped to No. 8 after a sweep at Bemidji State the following weekend. That set the stage for the final ever series with the University of Minnesota as WCHA league mates, at the National Hockey Center on Feb. 8-9. The Golden Gophers took the first game Friday, 4-2, with goals from Erik Haula and Nate Schmidt that broke a 2-2 tie in the third. Saturday's rematch was worthy of the final game in the rivalry with conference-standing implications. Four different players scored for SCSU, including tallies from Brodzinski and LeBlanc that gave the Huskies a 4-1 lead, but Nick Bjugstad and Nate Condon answered in the last half of the third period to make it a one-goal game. That's as close as they got, however, and Ryan Faragher made 36 saves for a 4-3 win and the split.

When the weekend ended, St. Cloud stood in first place in the WCHA with 31 points, three up on North Dakota with six games to play. The Gophers and Nebraska-Omaha were next with 26 points each, but Minnesota had two games "in hand" with eight to play while the other three had six each. What a fitting end to the WCHA chapter of SCSU's hockey history if it could win the MacNaughton Cup in its final season in the league. There was lots of work to do, however, before that could happen.

Minnesota picked up two points the following weekend while the Huskies and North Dakota were idle, winning Friday night in Madison before losing Sunday's reset with the Badgers outdoors at Soldier Field in Chicago. Omaha made the long trip to Anchorage and came home with a sweep and four points, leapfrogging into second place, only one point behind SCSU.

Still in control of their own fate, the Huskies had chances to seize the league championship outright several times in February and March. They came home from Colorado Springs with a hard-earned split against the Tigers on Feb. 22-23, and North Dakota did the same in Denver while in Minneapolis the Gophers split their final WCHA series with Minnesota-Duluth. With all four teams in action the first weekend of March, Omaha and UND entered the weekend tied with 30 points and the Gophers were two points behind first-place SCSU with 31. The Mavericks bowed out of the race with four straight losses, but Minnesota split its series with visiting Denver and North Dakota took three of four points at Ralph Engelstad Arena from Bemidji. A Huskies sweep in St. Cloud against Michigan Tech could have clinched a tie and guaranteed at least a share of the MacNaughton for the first time in school history, but after a 5-3 win Friday, the MTU Huskies blitzed the SCSU Huskies, 5-1, with Jimmy Murray scoring St. Cloud's only goal with 2:44 left to break up Jamie Phillips' shutout.

Nonetheless, they headed to Madison for the season's final weekend with a two-point lead over the Gophers and North Dakota, and with a win Friday still would clinch a tie. Those games were played at the Veterans Memorial Coliseum, formerly the Dane County Coliseum, where the Badgers played home

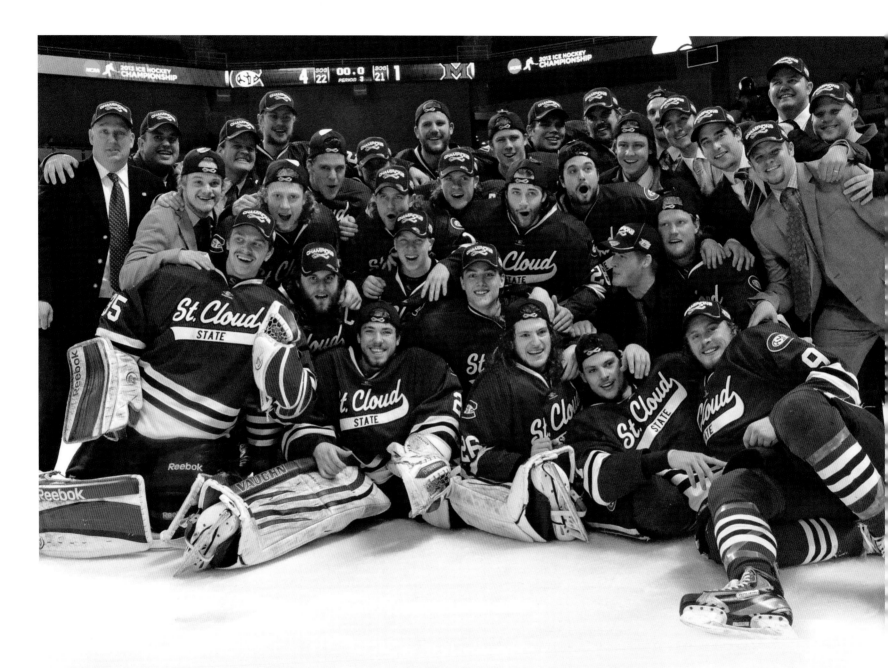

NCAA FROZEN FOUR 2013

games from 1967 to 1998, because their usual home arena at the Kohl Center was in use for the Wisconsin state basketball tournament. The Huskies trailed 2-1 heading into the final 20 minutes Friday before Jonny Brodzinski scored his second goal of the game 1:11 into the third to tie it, 2-2. Then with 3:35 left in the game, Nick Jensen netted his fourth of the season for a 3-2 lead, and captain LeBlanc salted it away with an empty-net marker in the final minute. Ryan Faragher made 26 saves and St. Cloud State's share of the league championship was secure.

The Gophers kept pace with a 4-3 win over the Beavers in Bemidji, and North Dakota did the same with a 4-3 win in Mankato — but now the best those two clubs could do was share the MacNaughton. Minnesota did its part with an easy 5-1 win Saturday, and as it turned out the MacNaughton was actually in Bemidji, and when the Badgers won Saturday's rematch with SCSU at the Old Dane, 3-2, the Gophers celebrated with the hardware. North Dakota lost in overtime, which meant the party wouldn't be any more crowded than it already was. Despite the tie, the Huskies got the No. 1 seed for the playoffs and celebrated a first-round sweep of Alaska-Anchorage by bringing the trophy on the ice, posing for pictures and reveling with their fans.

The Badgers started 2012-13 with only one win in their first 10 games and ended up sixth in the WCHA, but were playing their best hockey at the right time. They were arguably the hottest team in the league by the time they met St. Cloud in the semifinals at the Final Five on March 22. Wisconsin, back in their more familiar surroundings at the Kohl Center, had no trouble sweeping Minnesota-Duluth in their first-round series, then jumped all over Mankato in a Thursday play-in game at the Xcel, running out to a 4-0 lead — including two shorthanded goals — before Minnesota State got on the board a little past midway through the second. The Badgers went on to a 7-2 blowout win, earning the right to play SCSU in the first semifinal Friday afternoon.

The two teams traded goals in the first, with Ben Hanowski scoring on a man advantage for the Huskies, but John Ramage and Nic Kerdiles scored power-play goals of their own and Burnsville's Tyler Barnes sealed the deal with a goal into an empty net with 11 seconds left for a 4-1 Badgers win. On the other side of the bracket, Colorado College — also winners of a play-in game Thursday, over North Dakota — shut out the No. 2 seed, Minnesota, and for the first time in its history the WCHA Final Five championship would be contested by two teams that needed to win it in order to advance to the NCAA tournament. When the final horn sounded, Wisconsin was not to be denied, as the Badgers punched their ticket with a tight 3-2 win over the Tigers.

When the brackets for the NCAA tournament came out the next day, the Huskies learned they'd be heading east again — to Toledo, Ohio, as the No. 4 seed in the Midwest Regional, slotted below Minnesota State-Mankato (seeded third) and facing Notre Dame in the opener. Ben Hanowski scored the only goal of the first period, but after that the future was on full display in St. Cloud State's 5-1 waltz over the Fighting Irish. Joey Benik, who missed much of the early part of his freshman year after breaking his tibia in the team's first practice in the fall and didn't make his debut until just after Christmas, scored twice on power plays and assisted on Cory Thorson's goal in the second. Jonny Brodzinski scored SCSU's other goal with an assist from fellow rookie Jimmy Murray, and all told Huskies freshmen had six points in the game (three goals, three assists). Ryan Faragher had a relatively light afternoon in goal, needing just 17 saves to record the win.

Miami had no trouble with Mankato in the second game of the day, shutting out the Mavericks 4-0 and setting up a regional final matchup between the two future NCHC league mates Sunday. Once again it was the Joey Benik Show, as the freshman from St. Francis scored two more goals in a 4-1 win over the Redhawks. It was the fourth goal of the weekend for Benik, who scored only three the entire season heading into the weekend. He was the obvious choice as the regional's Most Outstanding Player. "It is hard to kind of be away from games that long," Benik, at the podium in front of the gathered press after the game, said of his three-month recovery from his early-season injury. "You just have to be ready and get into game shape, but you don't know what game shape is like until you're in the actual game... When I started to play games again, conditioning was (an adjustment)."

Blake Coleman scored Miami's only goal on a power play at the 7:50 mark of the second, a little more than 2 minutes after Benik's second goal made it 2-0. But Thorson answered just 2 minutes, 22 seconds after that and added his third goal of the weekend with an empty-net tally just before the final horn

Awards

Year	Player	Position	Team
1990-91	Bret Hedican	Defense	First
1992-93	Fred Knipscheer	Forward	First
1993-94	Kelly Hultgren	Defense	Second
1994-95	Kelly Hultgren	Defense	Second
1995-96	Taj Melson	Defense	Third
1996-97	Matt Cullen	Forward	Second
	Dave Paradise	Forward	Second
	Sacha Molin	Forward	Third
1997-98	Brian Leitza	Goaltender	Second
	Josh DeWolf	Defense	Third
1999-00	Mike Pudlick	Defense	First
	Tyler Arnason	Forward	Second
	Scott Meyer	Goaltender	Second
2000-01	Scott Meyer	Goaltender	First
	Duvie Wescott	Defense	Second
	Mark Hartigan	Forward	Third
	Brandon Sampair	Forward	Third
2001-02	Mark Hartigan	Forward	First
	Nate DiCasmirro	Forward	Second
	Dean Weasler	Goaltender	Second
2005-06	Bobby Goepfert	Goaltender	First
2006-07	Bobby Goepfert	Goaltender	First
	Andrew Gordon	Forward	First
	Andreas Nodl	Forward	Third
2007-08	Ryan Lasch	Forward	First
	Andreas Nodl	Forward	Second
	Garrett Roe	Forward	Second
2008-09	Ryan Lasch	Forward	First
	Garrett Raboin	Defense	Second
	Garrett Roe	Forward	Third
2009-10	Ryan Lasch	Forward	Second
	Dan Dunn	Goaltender	Third
	Garrett Raboin	Defense	Third
	Garrett Roe	Forward	Third
2010-11	Drew LeBlanc	Forward	Third
2011-12	Nick Jensen	Defense	Third
2012-13	Nick Jensen	Defense	First
	Drew LeBlanc	Forward	First

Taj Melson

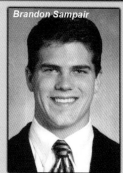
Brandon Sampair

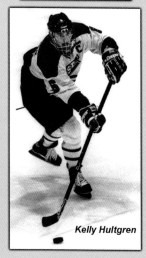
Kelly Hultgren

Sacha Molin

Andrew Gordon

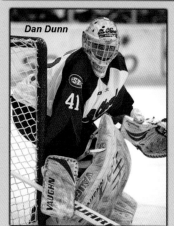
Dan Dunn

Dave Paradise

Josh DeWolf

Garrett Raboin

sounded. The Huskies once again played stout defense, and Faragher needed to make only 20 saves to anchor the third NCAA tournament victory in program history and send SCSU to the Frozen Four for the first time.

It turned out St. Cloud State had to wait just a tiny bit longer to make its NCAA Frozen Four debut. The first semifinal of the tournament, held Thursday, April 11, 2013, at CONSOL Energy Center — home rink of the NHL's Pittsburgh Penguins — went into overtime before a winner was decided. Yale, the third-place finisher in the ECAC, was the last team into the NCAA tournament after losing both its games at the league tournament three weeks before Pittsburgh. The Bulldogs had to wait until Sunday afternoon that weekend and sweat out the CCHA championship game between Notre Dame and Michigan. The math was simple: if the Wolverines won, claiming the CCHA's automatic bid, Yale's bubble was burst.

But the Irish prevailed and the Ivy Leaguers were in. Once included, Yale took full advantage, knocking off both Minnesota and North Dakota at the West Regional in Grand Rapids, Mich., to punch its own ticket to a truly unique Frozen Four. The Bulldogs, making the program's first appearance in the final four since 1952, met UMass-Lowell, who had snuffed out Wisconsin's tournament aspirations in the regionals, in the first national semifinal. The Riverhawks had been a Division II program until 1983 and were making only their fifth appearance ever in the Division I NCAA tourney. They'd never been to the Frozen Four before, nor had either team playing in the second semifinal, SCSU and Quinnipiac.

Lowell came out of the Northeast Regional as the No. 1 seed and was a trendy pick to win the tournament, but they were dominated by Yale in the first game of the day. The Bulldogs showed much more jump early and scored twice in the first for a 2-0 lead. The Riverhawks, outshot in every period — including 7-0 in overtime — rallied for two goals 14 seconds apart in the second period to tie it, and neither squad scored in the final 20 minutes. Finally senior Andrew Miller ended it at the 6:59 mark, and the Bulldogs were playing for a championship Saturday.

Once SCSU and Quinnipiac took to the ice for the night cap — about 45 minutes after the scheduled start time — the Huskies' hopes were dashed very quickly. The Bobcats got a power play barely a minute and a half into the first period and Jordan Samuels-Thomas converted 7 seconds into that man advantage, at the 1:49 mark. St. Cloud actually outshot its opponent 13-9 in the opening period, but goaltender Eric Hartzell, one of three Hobey Hat Trick finalists along with Drew LeBlanc, stopped all of them. Ryan Faragher, meanwhile, yielded goals on two of the first three shots he faced and three of nine in the first period, and the Huskies found themselves in a 3-0 hole after one.

Things played out pretty evenly from there, as both teams scored in the second — Joey Benik, again, for the Huskies — and SCSU held a two-shot advantage in the final 40 minutes (21-19), but the damage had been done. The Bobcats prevailed, 4-1, setting up an all-ECAC final and guaranteeing the league its first champion since Harvard beat Minnesota in overtime at the old St. Paul Civic Center in the 1989 title game. "I think we'd do anything to replay those first 11 minutes," coach Bob Motzko said at the postgame press conference. "That's probably the end of the story."

The team didn't come back to St. Cloud empty handed, however, as LeBlanc beat out Hartzell and Boston College star Johnny Gaudreau to become the 33rd winner of the Hobey Baker Award as college hockey's top player the Friday between the semifinals and championship. He became the first athlete to be named to the All-WCHA First Team, win the WCHA Player of the Year and WCHA Student-Athlete of the Year awards, and win the Hobey in the same season. He was only the second player named as the WCHA's top student athlete, joining defenseman Kyle McLaughlin in 1998-99. "I think (LeBlanc) winning the Hobey raised the profile of the program to another level," said *St. Cloud Times* hockey beat writer Mick Hatten. "If you look at the schools that previously had players win the award, they're programs that are typically among the best in the country."

LeBlanc led the nation with 37 assists in 42 games and finished with 105 assists for his career, second most in school history, behind only Garrett Roe's 113. His 147 career points rank sixth, but his place in the program's history as its first Hobey Baker winner and captain of its first Frozen Four team will never be matched. The same day he won the Hobey, the Chicago Blackhawks announced they had signed LeBlanc to a free-agent contract and he made his NHL debut with two games of action. He spent much of the rest of the spring along for the ride with the eventual Stanley Cup champs as one of the team's "Black Aces" —

Scholar-Athletes

Scholar-Athletes

2005-06	Nate Raduns
	Matt Stephenson
2006-07	Nate Raduns
2007-08	Jon Ammerman
	Brent Borgen
	Garrett Raboin
2008-09	Jon Ammerman
	Brent Borgen
	Nick Oslund
	Garrett Raboin
	Brian Volpei
2009-10	Jon Ammerman
	Jordy Christian
	Chris Hepp
	Drew LeBlanc
	Travis Novak
	Garrett Raboin
2010-11	Jordy Christian
	Oliver Lauridsen
	Drew LeBlanc
	Mike Lee
	Aaron Marvin
	Travis Novak
	Brian Volpei
2011-12	Jordy Christian
	Nic Dowd
	Kevin Gravel
	Nick Jensen
	Ben Hanowski
	Drew LeBlanc
	Mike Lee
	avis Novak
2012-13	Brooks Bertsch
	Nic Dowd
	Ryan Faragher
	Kevin Gravel
	Joey Holka
	Nick Jensen
	Drew LeBlanc
	David Morley
	Nick Oliver
	Joe Phillippi

Capital One Academic All-America

1998-99	Kyle McLaughlin (2nd Team)
2011-12	Mike Lee (1st Team)

Lowe's Senior Class All-America

2006-07	Nate Raduns (2nd Team)
2007-08	Marty Mjelleli (1st Team) - Finalist
2009-10	Garrett Raboin (1st Team)
2012-13	Ben Hanowski (2nd Team)

NCAA Elite 89 Award

2012-13	Brooks Bertsch

NCAA Elite 89™

Matt Stephenson

Jon Ammerman

2013 Premier Player of College Hockey Trophy

Marty Mjelleli

Nate Raduns

Bob Motzko-Coach, Brooks Bertsch
Heather Weems- Atheltic Director

Jordy Christian

David Morley

Travis Novak

minor leaguers traveling and practicing with the team but not playing in games. In between, he also suited up for six games with Team USA at the 2013 World Championships, playing part of the time early in the tournament on a line with former Gopher-turned Florida Panther Nick Bjugstad and coming home with a bronze medal. Both LeBlanc and Nick Jensen were named to the All-WCHA First Team, the first time since 2006-07 the Huskies had two players on the first unit (Bobby Goepfert and Andrew Gordon), and Jensen was named WCHA Defensive Player of the Year.

Jensen also turned pro, forgoing his final year of eligibility to sign with the team that drafted him in 2009, the Detroit Red Wings. Ben Hanowski, a Penguins draft pick traded to Calgary in the deal that sent Jarome Iginla to the Penguins just before the NCAA tourney began, signed with the Flames and scored his first goal in his NHL debut against the Wild on April 15 in Calgary. "I will always remember that week as being one of the best, yet most hectic and nerve-racking experiences of my hockey career. From playing in the Frozen Four to playing in the NHL against my hometown team, that time will always be special to me," Hanowski said.

While the players lost after that magical season were significant, most of the group was back as the Huskies embarked on the inaugural season of the National Collegiate Hockey Conference in 2013-14. The team's home rink, newly renamed the Herb Brooks National Hockey Center, underwent extensive renovations before the 2013-14 season in an effort to make for a more fan-friendly game-day experience. Upgrades included luxury suites, a large ticket atrium, and new décor including player murals, trophies, and banners. For the athletes, a new state-of-the-art locker room, training area and weight room were installed.

For many years the National Hockey Center, while a perfectly functional home arena, was not considered overly impressive, but now as one goes through the main entrance, it feels like you're walking into a big-time arena. Championship banners, murals and photos depicting the school's hockey history and tradition are everywhere. "My father looked at the opportunity to turn St. Cloud State into a Division I hockey program and took it on 110 percent," said Herb Brooks' son, Dan, at the grand re-opening of the new and improved National Hockey Center, now bearing his father's name. The school also honored Brooks' protégé, Craig Dahl, inducting the first coach of SCSU's Division I era into the St. Cloud State University Athletic Hall of Fame on Saturday, Oct. 12, 2013.

"Having facilities like we do at SCSU play a huge role in both the ability to recruit top-notch talent and develop that talent, which results in perennial winners," said Kirk Olson, a St. Cloud State alum and now the strength and conditioning coach for the Minnesota Wild.

It certainly has been quite a journey. From humble, simple and even unpolished beginnings the St. Cloud State program evolved into one of the best in college hockey, a step at a time with small incremental progress over decades. Having gone places and reached heights it never had before, the program started the new era in better form than at any time in its. Old rivalries aren't gone, now they're just different. And with a new league comes new rivalries that will grow and intensify over time. But the program has become something for the school and the community, and all of central Minnesota, to be proud of. "SCSU hockey belongs to St. Cloud," laments SCSU President Earl H. Potter III, who along with special athletics advisor Gino Gasparini actively worked to ensure the Huskies' inclusion in the new NCHC. "It is one of the most important ways in which the University and community are connected, and it's also the sport that calls out to the greatest number of students. Hockey brings us together."

WCHA Honors

WCHA Player of the Year

2001-02 Mark Hartigan
2012-13 Drew LeBlanc

WCHA Coach of the Year

1997-98 Craig Dahl
2005-06 Bob Motzko
2006-07 Bob Motzko

WCHA Rookie of the Year

2006-07 Andreas Nodl

WCHA All Rookie Team

1991-92 Sandy Gasseau
1994-95 Brian Leitza
1995-96 Matt Cullen
1998-99 Tyler Arnason
2001-02 Mike Doyle
         Matt Gens
         Peter Szabo
2006-07 Ryan Lasch
         Andreas Nodl
2007-08 Garrett Roe
2011-12 Andrew Prochno

WCHA Defenseman of the Year

2012-13 Nick Jensen

WCHA Scoring Champion

2001-02 Mark Hartigan
2007-03 Ryan Lasch

WCHA Student Athlete of the Year

1998-99 Kyle McLaughlin
2012-13 Drew LeBlanc

Craig Dahl | Matt Gens | Garrett Roe | Brian Leitza

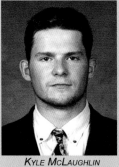

Mark Hartigan | Kyle McLaughlin | Andreas Nodl | Peter Szabo

Matt Cullen | Nick Jensen | Ryan Lasch | Mike Doyle

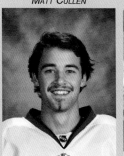

Andrew Prochno | Tyler Arnason | Bob Motzko | Drew LeBlanc

School Records

Games Played
1	Drew LeBlanc (2008-13)	171
2	Ryan Lasch (2006-10)	161
3	Nate Dey (2004-08)	159
4	Ben Hanowski (2009-13)	156
	Geno Parrish (1996-00)	156
	Garrett Raboin (2006-10)	156
	Garrett Roe (2007-11)	156
8	Aaron Marvin (2007-11)	154
	Joe Motzko (1999-03)	154
10	Several others tied	153

Garrett Roe

Goals
1	Mark Hartigan (1999-02)	86
2	Ryan Lasch (2006-10)	79
3	Jeff Saterdalen (1988-92)	78
4	Tim Hanus (1988-92)	73
	Chris Scheid (1987-91)	73
6	Dave Paradise (1993-97)	66
7	Garrett Roe (2007-11)	65
8	Tyler Arnason (1998-01)	61
9	Fred Knipscheer (1990-93)	58
10	Ryan Malone (1999-03)	56

Assists
1	Garrett Roe (2007-11)	113
2	Drew LeBlanc (2008-13)	105
3	Ryan Lasch (2006-10)	104
4	Jeff Saterdalen (1988-92)	101
5	Tim Hanus (1988-92)	99
6	Joe Motzko (1999-03)	90
7	Nate DiCasmirro (1998-02)	85
8	Ryan Malone (1999-03)	84
9	Brandon Sampair (1997-01)	80
10	Mark Hartigan (1999-02)	79
	Kelly Hultgren (1991-95)	79

Ryan Lasch with Jeff Saterdalen

Points in a Career
1	Ryan Lasch (2006-10)	183
2	Jeff Saterdalen (1988-92)	179
3	Garrett Roe (2007-11)	178
4	Tim Hanus (1988-92)	172
5	Mark Hartigan (1999--02)	165
6	Drew LeBlanc (2008-13)	147
7	Joe Motzko (1999-03)	142
8	Ryan Malone (1999-03)	140
9	Tyler Arnason (1998-01)	136
	Nate DiCasmirro (1998-02)	136

Penalty Minutes
1	Dave Paradise (1993-97)	297
2	Tony Gruba (1990-94)	295
3	Ryan Malone (1999-03)	281
4	Kelly Hultgren (1991-95)	257
5	Dan Reimann (1992-96)	252
6	Garrett Roe (2007-11)	240
7	Mike Notermann (1987-91)	236
8	Jeff Finger (2000-03)	235
9	Chris Hepp (2008-11)	224
10	Sandy Gasseau (1991-95)	218

Games Played Goaltending
1	Brian Leitza (1994-98)	133
2	Mike O'Hara (1988-92)	98
3	Grant Sjerven (1991-94)	89
4	Scott Meyer (1996-01)	80
5	Mike Lee (2009-12)	74
	Dean Weasler (1998-02)	74
7	Bobby Goepfert (2005-07)	73
	Jase Weslosky (2006-09)	73
9	Ryan Faragher (2011-present)	63
10	Tim Boron (2003-06)	53

Goals Against Average
1	Bobby Goepfert (2005-07)	2.24
2	Scott Meyer (1996-01)	2.38
3	Ryan Faragher (2011-present)	2.52
4	Dean Weasler (1998-02)	2.63
5	Mike Lee (2009-12)	2.65
6	Jase Weslosky (2006-09)	2.68
7	Dan Dunn (2007-11)	2.72
8	Jake Moreland (1999-03)	2.79
9	Adam Coole (2003-04)	2.82
10	Jason Montgomery (2002-06)	2.96

Mike O'Hara

Wins
1	Brian Leitza (1994-98)	66
2	Scott Meyer (1996-01)	47
3	Grant Sjerven (1991-94)	39
	Dean Weasler (1998-02)	39
5	Bobby Goepfert (2005-07)	37
	Mike O'Hara (1988-92)	37
	Jase Weslosky (2006-09)	37
8	Ryan Faragher (2011-present)	33
9	Mike Lee (2009-12)	32
10	Jake Moreland (1999-03)	26

Save Percentage
1	Bobby Goepfert (2005-07)	.924
2	Jase Weslosky (2006-09)	.920
3	Scott Meyer (1996-01)	.919
4	Mike Lee (2009-12)	.917
5	Ryan Faragher (2011-present)	.915
6	Dean Weasler (1998-02)	.914
7	Jake Moreland (1999-03)	.910
8	Dan Dunn (2007-11)	.907
9	Adam Coole (2003-04)	.902
10	Jason Montgomery (2002-06)	.899

Grant Sjevern

Shutouts
1	Scott Meyer (1996-01)	9
2	Dean Weasler (1998-02)	7
3	Bobby Goepfert (2005-07)	6
	Brian Leitza (1994-98)	6
	Jase Weslosky (2006-09)	6
6	Grant Sjerven (1991-94)	5
7	Ryan Faragher (2011-present)	4
	Mike Lee (2009-12)	4
	Jake Moreland (1999-03)	4
10	Mike O'Hara (1988-92)	2

Jase Weslosky

NCAA All-Americans

#2 Rory Eidsness
1ST TEAM WEST
GOALIE
SEASON 1981-82

HOMETOWN: FARGO, ND

#1 Scott Meyer
2ND TEAM WEST
GOALIE
SEASON 2000-01

HOMETOWN: RUGBY, ND

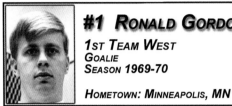

#1 RONALD GORDON
1ST TEAM WEST
GOALIE
SEASON 1969-70

HOMETOWN: MINNEAPOLIS, MN

#20 Dan Pratt
1ST TEAM WEST
DEFENSE
SEASON 1981-82

HOMETOWN: MINNEAPOLIS, MN

#3 Mark Hartigan
1ST TEAM WEST
FORWARD
SEASON 2001-02

HOMETOWN: FORT ST. JOHN, BC

#12 PAUL OBERSTAR
1ST TEAM WEST
FORWARD
SEASON 1970-71

HOMETOWN: HIBBING, MN

#20 Mike Brodzinski
1ST TEAM WEST
FORWARD
SEASON 1985-86 AND 1986-87

HOMETOWN: PHILADELPHIA, PA

#47 Bobby Goepfert
2ND TEAM WEST
GOALIE
SEASON 2005-06 AND 2006-07

HOMETOWN: KINGS PARK, NY

#9 John Fitzsimmons
1ST TEAM WEST
FORWARD
SEASON 1972-73

HOMETOWN: ROSEVILLE, MN

#7 FRED KNIPSCHEER
2ND TEAM WEST
FORWARD
SEASON 1992-93

HOMETOWN: FT. WAYNE, IN

#19 Ryan Lasch
2ND TEAM WEST
FORWARD
SEASON 2007-08

HOMETOWN: LAKE FOREST, CA

#21 Pat Sullivan
1ST TEAM WEST
FORWARD
SEASON 1973-74 AND 1974-75

HOMETOWN: CROOKSTON, MN

#21 Mark Parrish
2ND TEAM WEST
FORWARD
SEASON 1996-97

HOMETOWN: BLOOMINGTON, MN

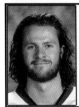

#14 Nick Jensen
1ST TEAM WEST
DEFENSE
SEASON 2012-13

HOMETOWN: ROGERS, MN

#8 Dave Reichel
1ST TEAM WEST
FORWARD
SEASON 1977-78 AND 1978-79

HOMETOWN: HOPKINS, MN

#22 Mike Pudlick
2ND TEAM WEST
DEFENSE
SEASON 1999-00

HOMETOWN: BLAINE, MN

#19 Drew LeBlanc
1ST TEAM WEST
FORWARD
SEASON 2012-13

HOMETOWN: HERMANTOWN, MN

Hobey Baker Memorial Award

Bobby Goepfert

Ryan Lasch   Coach Eric Rud

Mark Hartigan

These standouts Huskies were recognized among the nation's top collegiate players,
shown here at the Hobey Baker Award Banquet for their respected year of nomination.

Hobey Baker

Character Builds Excellence

Hobey Baker Finalist	
Mark Hartigan	2002
Bobby Goepfert	2007
Ryan Lasch	2008
Drew LeBlanc	2013

The Hobey Baker Award is a prestigious honor given each April to the NCAA men's hockey player that demonstrates outstanding sportsmanship and fair play. Hobey Baker was a man that despised foul play and received only two penalties in his entire college career at Princeton University. He exemplified the skills necessary to be an outstanding player; his speed and stickhandling set new standards for aspiring stars. His dedication to his beliefs were also demonstrated when he served and gave his life for his country as an American pilot in World War I.

Hobey Baker Memorial Award Winner

DREW LeBLANC, a senior from Hermantown, Minnesota, led the nation with 37 assists in 42 games, while also scoring 13 goals to finish with 50 points in 2012-13. The two-time captain was a creative play-making center with uncanny vision and the ability to slow the game down, making him an exciting player to watch.

Drew capped his career at St. Cloud with 42 goals and 105 assists, totalling 147 points in a school-record 171 games played.

His exemplary play and leadership helped the Huskies reach the NCAA Frozen Four in Pittsburgh in 2013.

Throwing out the "first pitch" for a Minnesota Twins game

Drew with his teammates at Target Field being honored for receiving the prestigious Premier Player Award 2013

Guest appearance at the ESPN ESPYs Awards Show in Los Angeles

World Juniors

Mike Lee

Mark Parrish

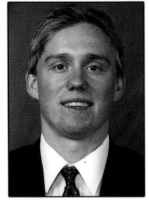

Peter Szabo

Casey Borer

Kevin Gravel

John Perpich	Coach	1983, 1984	USA	
Tony Burns	Defense	1991	USA	
Matt Cullen	Forward	1996	USA	
Mark Parrish	Forward	1996, 1997	USA	Silver '97
Peter Szabo	Forward	2001	Slovakia	
Bobby Goepfert	Goaltender	2003	USA	
Mike Eaves	Coach	2004	USA	Gold
Mike Hastings	Coach	2004, 2006	USA	Gold '04
Andreas Nodl	Forward	2004	Austria	
Casey Borer	Defense	2005	USA	
Mike Gibbons	Coach	2006	USA	
John Harrington	Coach	2007	USA	
Oliver Lauridsen	Defense	2008	Denmark	
Mike Lee	Goaltender	2010	USA	Gold
Kevin Gravel	Defense	2012	USA	
Rikard Gronborg	Coach	2012, 2013, 2014	Sweden	Gold '12
Bob Motzko	Coach	2014	USA	

Andreas Nodl

Mike Gibbons

Mike Lee

Mike Hastings

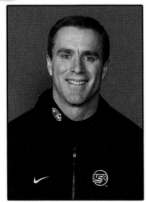

Mike Eaves

World Championships

Drew LeBlanc

Josh DeWolf

Ryan Lasch

Ryan Malone

Name	Position	Years	Country	Medal
Herb Brooks	Coach	1979, 1998	USA & France	
Mike Eaves	Coach	1991, 2006	USA	
Len Esau	Defense	1995	Canada	Bronze
Bret Hedican	Defense	1997, 1999, 2001	USA	
Matt Cullen	Forward	1998, 1999, 2003, 2004	USA	Bronze '04
Mark Parrish	Forward	1998, 2001, 2005	USA	
Josh DeWolf	Defense	2002	USA	
Gert Prohaska	Goaltender	2002, 2003	Austria	
Ryan Malone	Forward	2004, 2006	USA	Bronze '04
Mike Pudlick	Defense	2004	USA	Bronze
Tyler Arnason	Forward	2007	USA	
Andreas Nodl	Forward	2009	Austria	
John Harrington	Coach	2011	Slovenia	
Rikard Gronborg	Coach	2012, 2013	Sweden	Gold '13
Ryan Lasch	Forward	2012	USA	
Oliver Lauridsen	Defense	2013	Denmark	
Drew LeBlanc	Forward	2013	USA	Bronze

Rikard Gronborg

Oliver Lauridsen

Matt Cullen

Len Esau

Gert Prohaska

OLYMPIANS FROM SCSU

BRET HEDICAN, MATT CULLEN & MARK PARRISH - 2006 WINTER GAMES IN TORINO, ITALY

Olympians from St. Cloud State

Name	Pos	Year	Team
Herb Brooks*	Coach	1980 - Lake Placid	USA
John Harrington*	Player	1980 - Lake Placid	USA
John Harrington*	Coach	1984 - Sarajevo	USA
Bret Hedican	D	1992 - Albertville	USA
Herb Brooks*	Coach	1998 - Nagano	FRA
Herb Brooks*	Coach	2002 - Salt Lake	USA
Matt Cullen	F	2006 - Torino	USA
Bret Hedican	D	2006 - Torino	USA
Mark Parrish	F	2006 - Torino	USA
Ryan Malone	F	2010 - Vancouver	USA
Rikard Gronborg	Coach	2014 - Sochi	SWE

*Coach at SCSU only

RYAN MALONE CAPTURES THE SIVER MEDAL
AT THE 2010 WINTER GAMES IN VANCOUVER

Herb Brooks Coach
of 1980 "Miracle on Ice"

St. Cloud State NHL Draft Picks

Mike Lee and Ben Hanowski athe the 2009 NHL Entry Draft.

Player	Team	Year	Round	Overall Pick
Tony Schmalzbauer	New York Islanders	1986	6	122
Tim Hanus	Quebec Nordiques	1987	7	135
Jeff Saterdalen	New York Islanders	1987	7	160
Dan Brettschneider	Washington Capitals	1987	12	240
Lenny Esau	Toronto Maple Leafs	1988	5	86
Jeff Kruesel	Los Angeles Kings	1988	7	133
Jon Pojar	Chicago Blackhawks	1988	8	155
Shorty Forrest	New York Islanders	1988	9	173
Bret Hedican	St. Louis Blues	1988	10	198
Joe Larson	Winnipeg Jets	1989	10	193
Greg Hagen	Pittsburgh Penguins	1989	10	205
Noel Rahn	Quebec Nordiques	1989	12	252
Tony Burns	Detroit Red Wings	1990	5	87
Tony Gruba	Detroit Red Wings	1990	9	171
Brett Lievers	New York Rangers	1990	11	223
Bill Lund	Philadelphia Flyers	1990	12	235
Eric Johnson	Vancouver Canucks	1991	8	161
Jay Moser	Boston Bruins	1991	8	172
Dan Reimann	New Jersey Devils	1991	9	187
P.J. Lepler	Montreal Canadiens	1991	11	237
Dan O'Shea	Minnesota North Stars	1991	5	14
Jason Stewart	New York Islanders	1994	6	142
Brian Leitza	Pittsburgh Penguins	1994	11	284
Mike Rucinski	Hartford Whalers	1995	8	217
Matt Cullen	Anaheim Mighty Ducks	1996	2	35
Josh DeWolf	New Jersey Devils	1996	2	41
Mark Parrish	Colorado Avalanche	1996	3	79
Brian Gaffaney	Pittsburgh Penguins	1997	2	44
Tyler Arnason	Chicago Blackhawks	1998	7	183
Ryan Malone	Pittsburgh Penguins	1999	4	115
Doug Meyer	Pittsburgh Penguins	1999	6	176
Jeff Finger	Colorado Avalanche	1999	8	240
Matt Hendricks	Nashville Predators	2000	5	131
Brock Hooton	Ottawa Senators	2002	5	150
Bobby Goepfert	Pittsburgh Penguins	2002	6	171
Tim Conboy	San Jose Sharks	2002	7	217
Matt Gens	Vancouver Canucks	2002	9	278

Player	Team	Year	Round	Overall Pick
Jonathan Lehun	St. Louis Blues	2003	6	189
Joe Jensen	Pittsburgh Penguins	2003	8	232
Casey Borer	Carolina Hurricanes	2004	3	89
Andrew Gordon	Washington Capitals	2004	7	197
Andreas Nodl	Philadelphia Flyers	2006	2	39
Jase Weslosky	New York Islanders	2006	4	108
Nick Oslund	Detroit Red Wings	2006	7	191
Aaron Marvin	Calgary Flames	2007	3	89
Dan Dunn	Washington Capitals	2007	6	154
Garrett Roe	Los Angeles Kings	2008	7	183
Ben Hanowski	Pittsburgh Penguins	2009	3	63
Mike Lee	Phoenix Coyotes	2009	3	91
Nick Oliver	Nashville Predators	2009	4	110
Nick Jensen	Detroit Red Wings	2009	5	150
Cam Reid	Nashville Predators	2009	7	192
Oliver Lauridsen	Philadelphia Flyers	2009	7	196
Nic Dowd	Los Angeles Kings	2009	7	209
Kevin Gravel	Los Angeles Kings	2010	5	148
Judd Peterson	Buffalo Sabres	2012	7	204
Jonny Brodzinski	Los Angeles Kings	2013	5	148
Ben Storm	Colorado Avalanche	2013	6	153

Huskies in the NHL

Andrew Gordon

Bret Hedican

Ben Hanowski

Matt Cullen

Joe Jensen

Casey Borer

Len Esau

Drew LeBlanc

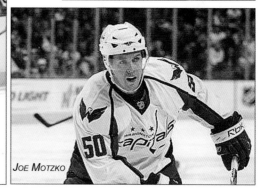

Joe Motzko

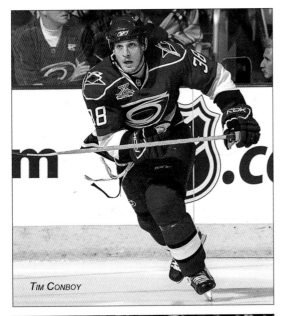

Tim Conboy

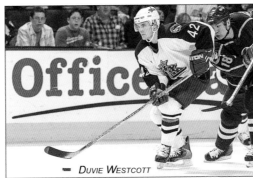

Duvie Westcott

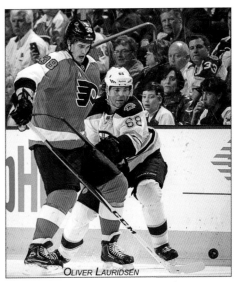

Oliver Lauridsen

Mark Parrish

Tyler Arnason

Ryan Malone

Matt Hendricks

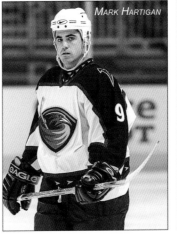

Mark Hartigan

Steve Martinson

Fred Knipscheer

Jeff Finger

Frank Brimsek

Scott Meyer

Andreas Nodl

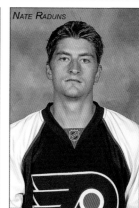

Nate Raduns

Sam LoPresti

NHL Coaches

Mikes Eaves

Herb Brooks

John Perpich

NHL Awards and Hall of Fame

Hockey Hall Of Fame

Frank Brimsek	Player	1966
Herb Brooks	Coach	2006

USA Hockey Hall of Fame

Frank Brimsek	Player	1973
Sam LoPresti	Player	1973
Herb Brooks	Player	1990
Sergio Gambucci	Coach	1996

Stanley Cup Champions

Frank Brimsek	Boston Bruins	1938-39
Frank Brimsek	Boston Bruins	1940-41
Matt Cullen	Carolina Hurricanes	2005-06
Bret Hedican	Carolina Hurricanes	2005-06
Mark Hartigan	Anaheim Ducks	2006-07
Joe Motzko	Anaheim Ducks	2006-07
Mark Hartigan	Detroit Red Wings	2007-08

NHL All-Star Team Selections

(1st Team/2nd Team)

Frank Brimsek	Boston Bruins (1st)	1938-39
Frank Brimsek	Boston Bruins (2nd)	1939-40
Frank Brimsek	Boston Bruins (2nd)	1940-41
Frank Brimsek	Boston Bruins (1st)	1941-42
Frank Brimsek	Boston Bruins (2nd)	1942-43
Frank Brimsek	Boston Bruins (2nd)	1945-46
Frank Brimsek	Boston Bruins (2nd)	1946-47
Frank Brimsek	Boston Bruins (2nd)	1947-48

Lester Patrick Trophy

(Contributer to USA hockey)

Herb Brooks	Team USA	2001-02

Vezina Trophy

(Best Goaltender)

Frank Brimsek	Boston Bruins	1938-39
Frank Brimsek	Boston Bruins	1941-42

Calder Memorial Trophy

(Rookie of the Year)

Frank Brimsek	Boston Bruins	1938-39

NHL All-Rookie Team

Tyler Arnason	Chicago Blackhawks	2002-03
Ryan Malone	Pittsburgh Penguins	2003-04

AHL Champions

Frank Brimsek	Providence Reds	1937-38
Sam LoPresti	St. Paul Saints	1938-39
Brett Lievers	Utah Grizzlies	1995-96
Joe Motzko	Chicago Wolves	1997-98
Matt Hendricks	Milwaukee Admirals	2003-04
Andrew Gordon	Hershey Bears	2008-09
Andrew Gordon	Hershey Bears	2009-10

AHL All-Star Team Selections

(1st Team/2nd Team)

Sam LoPresti	St. Paul Saints (2nd)	1938-39
Andrew Gordon	Hershey Bears (2nd)	2009-10

AHL Rookie of the Year

Tyler Arnason	Norfolk Admirals	2001-02

AHL All-Rookie Team

Tyler Arnason	Norfolk Admirals	2001-02

Fred T. Hunt Trophy

(AHL Sportsmanship)

Casey Borer	Albany River Rats	2009-10

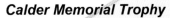

Sergio Gambucci

Matt Cullen

Joe Motzko

Andrew Gordon

Mark Hartigan

Bret Hedican

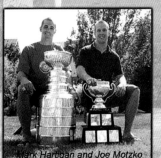
Mark Hartigan and Joe Motzko

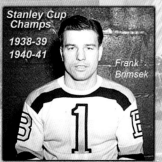
Stanley Cup Champs
1938-39
1940-41
Frank Brimsek

SCSU Hockey
Team Photos

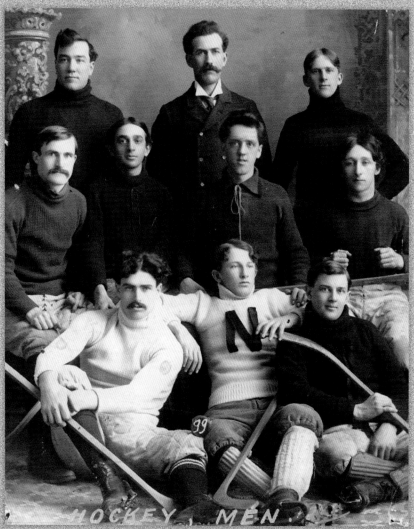

HOCKEY MEN.

1899

1931-32

1932-33

1933-34

1934-35

1935-36

1936-37

1937-38

1938-39

1939-40

1940-41

1941-42

1947-48

1948-49

1949-50

1950-51

1951-52

1952-53

1953-54

1954-55

1955-56

1956-57

1957-58

1958-59

1959-60

1961-62

1962-63

1963-64

1964-65

1965-66

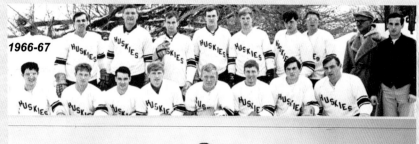

1966-67

1967-68

1974-75

1975-76

NO SMOKING
IN BLEACHERS

1977-78

1978-79

1979-80

1980-81

1981-82

1982-83

1983-84

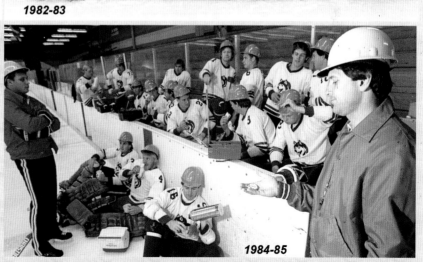

1984-85

1986-87

1987-88

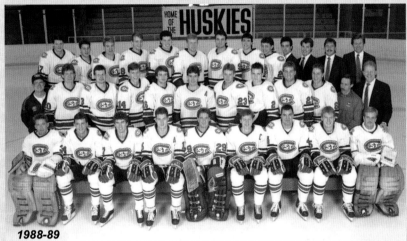

1988-89

1990-91

1991-92

1992-93

1993-94

1994-95

1995-96

1996-97

1997-98

1998-99

1999-00

2000-01

2001-02

2002-03

2003-04

2004-05

2005-06

2006-07

2007-08

2008-09

2009-10

2010-11

2011-12

2012-13

HUSKIES   HUSKIES   HUSKIES!!!

SCSU Hockey
All-Time Roster

Absey, John	1957-58	Benik, Joey	2012-	Burrell, Brandon	2010-14	DiCasmirro, Nate	1998-02
Ackerman, Shawn	1979-80	Bergo, John	1980-84			Dick, Jim	1986-87
Adamic, Gerald	1947-50	Berkowitz, Mike	1940-41	Caple, Jim	1987-88	Dierbeck, Darren	1987-89
Ahles, Bob	1952-54	Bertsch, Brooks	2011-	Carey, Pat	1965-66	Dingle, John	1978-79
Albright, Dave	1958-59	Best, Randy	1993-97	Carlisle, David	2005-09	Dockry, Kevin	1985-86
Alden, Louis	1932-33	Bianchi, Tony	1989-90	Carlson, Bill	1955-56	Doherty, Tim	1973-77
Alexander, James	1932-35	Bifulk, Archie	1998-00	Carmichael, Dale	1960-64	Donovan, John	1978-80
Alexander, Joe	1978-82	Bitter, Curt	1984-86	Carroll, Jack	1967-68	Dornack, Dean	1976-78
Alexander, John	1932-36	Bizal, Brady	1983-84	Cedarholm, Charles	1947, 54	Dornfeld, Tom	1972-76
Alexander, Mark	1986-87	Bizal, Terry	1982-86	Champa, Ludwig	1935-37	Dowd, Nic	2010-14
Allen, Harry	1952-53	Bjork, Bernard	1932-35	Charbonneau, Paul	1985-86	Doyle, Mike	2001-05
Alm, Tony	1967-68	Bjorkland, Tic	1949-51	Chartier, Scott	1986-90	Doyle, Pete	1976-77
Almer, Ken	1968-70	Bjorklund, Ralph	1932-34	Charzan, Dennis	1976-78	Duncan, Jim	1962-63
Ammerman, Jon	2006-10	Bleyhl, David	1967-69	Checco, Tom	1962-63	Duncan, John	1961-64
Amundson, Clayton	1937-40	Bloom, Gene	1958-59	Chillgren, Randolph	1940-41	Dunn, Dan	2007-11
Anderson, Bill	1941-42	Boche, John	1983-84	Chisholm, John	1982-83	Durain, Chris	1966-67
Anderson, Chris	2004-08	Boe, Ron	1972-75	Christian, Jordy	2008-12	Dwyer, Aaron	1998-00
Anderson, Dave	1967-69	Bohn, Theodore	1932-33	Christian, Ryan	1986-87	
Anderson, Dick	1959-60	Booker, Denis	1936-37	Clafton, Grant	2003-07	Eastman, Derek	1999-03
Anderson, Dick	1949-51	Borer, Casey	2003-07	Cleven, Randy	1963-64	Eddy, David	2009-12
Anderson, Edward	1931-32	Borgen, Brent	2007-09	Clunis, Kevin	1976-80	Edelstein, Paul	1979-83
Anderson, George	1936-38	Boron, Tim	2003-06	Conboy, Tim	2002-04	Eichstadt, Scott	1987-91
Anderson, Jim	1981-85	Bouchard, Paul	1955-56	Cook, Brian	1987-91	Eidsness, Rory	1979-80
Anderson, Keith	1997-01	Boughen, Ralph	1958-59	Coole, Adam	2003-04	Elmquist, Wayne	1968-69
Anderson, Phil	1958-59	Braga, Al	1947-48	Cooper, Dan	1969-71	Empey, Steve	1966-68
Anderson, Tom	1980-81	Brandt, Bill	1963-66	Cooper, Neil	1992-94	Engstrom, Rick	1979-80
Andreasson, Butch	1965-66	Brandt, Pete	1966-67	Coppock, Bill	1966-67	Erickson, Charles	1935-36
Armstrong, Larry	1947-48	Branham, Terry	1966-67	Couture, Leigh	1958-59	Erickson, Don	1954-55
Arnason, Tyler	1998-01	Brettschneider, Dan	1987-88	Cox, Duane	1955-56	Erickson, Louis	1935-39
Arnold, Bob	1988-90	Brimsek, Frank	1933-34	Cullen, Jon	1999-03	Erksine, Roger	1959-61
Awada, George	1995-99	Brocklehurst, Aaaron	2004-08	Cullen, Matt	1995-97	Esau, Len	1988-90
Ayers, Steve	1981-83	Broderick, Bernard	1936-40			Ethen, Bob	1970-72
		Brodt, Vic	1986-90	Dahl, Norman	1957-58	Etienne, Les	1958-62
Bailey, Matt	1996-00	Brodzinski, Jonny	2012-	Daly, Tim	2011-14	Etnier, John	1965-69
Bailey, Wayne	1937-38	Brodzinski, Mike	1984-87	DelCastillo, Doc	1988-92	Evans, Charles	1940-41
Barger, Mark	1988-89	Brodzinski, Steve	1984-87	Delisle, Steve	1979-81	
Barta, Brett	2007-11	Brooks, Lee	1998-02	DeMike, Nick	1958-59	Fairchild, Cory	1991-93
Baumann, Steve	1972-73	Browning, Tim	1968-69	DePaul, Arnold	1940-42	Faragher, Ryan	2011-
Baxter, Jim	1954-56	Brynstad, Denny	1955-59	DePaul, Robert	1934-35	Fazio, Dave	1981-82
Beaudet, Dick	1963-64	Bucholz, Jim	1982-83	DePaul, Walter	1933-35	Fertig, Sheldon	1953-55
Becht, Doug	1972-73	Burke, Jack	1959-63	DeWolf, Josh	1996-98	Festler, Jared	2008-12
Belisle, T.J.	2012-	Burns, Tony	1990-92	Dey, Nate	2004-08	Finger, Jeff	2000-03

Finnegan, Herm	1986-90	Goepfert, Bobby	2005-07	Hartman, Matt	2004-08	Johnson, Bryce	2010-11
Finnerty, Mike	1987-88	Goodrich, Bob	1952-53	Hassler, Les	1968-69	Johnson, Eric	1991-95
Fitzsimmons, John	1969-73	Googins, Roger	1960-62	Hastings, Mike	1986-88	Johnson, Paul	1973-75
Fitzsimmons, Mike	1959-60	Goral, Don	1971-72	Hawkinson, Skeeter	1960-63	Johnson, Ron	1980-84
Fitzsimmons, Tom	1976-77	Gordon, Andrew	2004-07	Hedican, Bret	1988-91	Johnson, Ryan	2000-02
Fletcher, Justin	2003-07	Gordon, Ron	1968-69	Heitke, Clifford	1935-36	Johnson, Taylor	2009-13
Forbes, Ryan	1998-99	Goslin, Leo	1954-56	Heitke, Frederick	1935-36	Juran, Jim	1967-68
Forrest, Shorty	1986-88	Goulet, Brad	1995-99	Hemberger, Bob	1949-50		
Forsberg, Eugene	1951-55	Goulet, Jason	1995-99	Hemberger, Dick	1950-54	Kahaly, Arnie	1954-55
Fountain, Ron	1960-61	Goulet, Terry	1976-77	Hendricks, Matt	2000-04	Kangas, Don	1948-50
Fowler, Jim	1983-85	Govednik, Marty	1939-42	Hengen, Billy	2002-06	Kauppi, Clifford	1934-36
Francis, Matt	2004-06	Grant, Bob	1949-51	Hepp, Chris	2008-11	Kearney, Joe	1963-64
Frantti, Bill	1950-52	Grant, Wally	1969-71	Higgins, Bob	1960-64	Kearney, Phillip	1935-36
Fredricks, Mike	1958-60	Gravel, Jim	1977-81	Hilgert, Tom	1967-68	Kellogg, Steve	1970-74
Freeburg, Bucky	1958-60	Gravel, Kevin	2010-14	Hill, Brent	2003-04	Kennedy, Bill	1957-59
French, Monte	1985-86	Grimes, Bill	1947-49	Hiti, Louie	1948-50	Kennedy, Eloy	1941-42
Frisch, Ryan	1995-99	Gronberg, Rikard	1989-92	Holka, Joey	2011-	Kennedy, Todd	1988-92
Fritsinger, Bill	1958-62	Gruba, Tony	1990-94	Hollenhorst, Carl	1934-35	Kissner, Gary	1979-80
		Grund, Ken	1963-64	Hollenhorst, Rudolph	1931-33	Klasnick, Rob	1994-98
Gaffaney, Brian	1997-01	Gumaelius, Petter	1995-96	Holt, Todd	1984-87	Klinger, John	1983-87
Gagnon, Marc	1992-95	Gustafson, Charley	1952-53	Holum, Dave	1991-95	Knipscheer, Fred	1990-93
Gale, A.J.	2006-08	Gustafson, Steve	1967-68	Hooton, Brock	2002-06	Koch, Henry	1932-34
Gambucci, Sergio	1947-48			Hoover, Dave	1980-83	Koob, Tom	1963-64
Garrity, Sean	2004-06	Haataja, Steve	1987-91	Houseman, Gary	2003-07	Korfhage, Bill	1984-88
Gasperlin, Al	1938-39	Hackett, Doug	1984-85	Houtz, John	1952-56	Korpela, Andy	1972-75
Gasperlin, Ray	1932-35	Hackett, Nick	1984-85	Huffer, Bruce	1970-71	Korsman, Tom	1974-75
Gasseau, Sandy	1991-95	Hagen, Greg	1990-93	Hughes, Mark	1973-75	Kossila, Kalle	2012-
Gaudet, Craig	2006-10	Hagen, Mark	1983-85	Hultgren, Kelly	1991-95	Kotary, Mark	1994-95
Gayman, Wally	1965-66	Hajostek, Mike	1979-83	Humeniuk, Jim	1961-64	Kottke, Lawrence	1937-41
Geisbauer, Jay	1992-96	Hall, Tom	1958-61	Hunter, Dan	1976-79	Kraushaar, Greg	1972-73
Gens, Matt	2001-05	Haller, D.J.	1985-87			Kreager, Jim	1971-73
Gens, Phil	1960-63	Halstead, Jim	1956-57	Iannazzo, Dave	2001-05	Kronick, Dan	2005-07
Gerzin, Walter	1935-38	Hanna, Adam	2002-03	Irwin, Wally	1956-60	Kruchten, John	1976-79
Gherardi, Rich	1983-85	Hanowski, Ben	2009-13			Kuzara, Jeff	1987-91
Giachino, Brian	1988-89	Hanson, Harold	1931-32	Jacobs, Harold	1935-36		
Gilbertson, Dale	1979-82	Hanson, John	1959-60	Jacobson, Steve	1971-73	Laine, Don	1962-63
Gilbertson, Gilbert	1963-64	Hanus, Tim	1988-92	Janski, Mel	1947-48	LaMere, Ryan	2000-04
Gilkinson, Alan	1948-51	Hardy, Nate	2008-12	Jaskowiak, Blake	1947-50	Lane, John	1938-40
Gill, Bob	1947-48	Harjung, Bruce	1963-64	Jensen, Joe	2002-06	LaRoque, Bruce	1984-87
Gingerich, Dave	1989-90	Harmala, Joe	1963-64	Jensen, Nick	2010-13	Larson, Bill	1962-66
Glines, Marlon	1972-76	Harold, Mike	1951-52	Jiskra, Jason	1994-95	Larson, Garrett	2001-04
Goehrs, William	1931-33	Hartigan, Mark	1999-02	Johnson, Bob	1969-70	Larson, Joe	1989-90

Larson, Ritchie	1997-00	Macken, Bryce	1996-00	Meyer, Doug	2001-02	O'Connell, Mike	1993-97
Larson, Vern	1954-56	MacMillan, Mitch	2010-12	Meyer, Scott	1996-01	O'Hara, Mike	1988-92
Lasch, Ryan	2006-10	Malone, Ryan	1999-03	Miggins, Bob	1958-59	Oliver, Nick	2011-
Lau, Doug	1972-73	Manthey, Todd	1985-86	Milan, Garrett	2011-	Olsen, Bernard	1936-38
Lauridsen, Oliver	2008-11	Maristuen, Mike	1993-98	Miller, Bob	1973-75	Olson, Gordy	1950-51
LaVigne, Pete	1977-78	Markstrom, Chris	1992-95	Miller, Paul	1984-86	Olson, Harry	1959-62
Leary, Pat	1968-69	Marlow, Jim	1978-82	Miller, Paul	1971-73	Olson, Michael	2005-09
LeBlanc, Drew	2008-13	Maroney, Dave	1974-75	Misnor, Harvey	1957-58	O'Malley, Edward	1936-37
LeClair, Rich	1955-56	Martin, Donald	1932-34	Mjelleli, Marty	2004-08	Osen, Paul	1990-91
Lecy, Mark	1976-79	Martin, George	1951-53	Molin, Sacha	1995-98	O'Shea, Dan	1989-93
LeDoux, Harley	1935-40	Martin, Jim	1959-60	Montgomery, Jason	2001-06	Oslund, Nick	2007-11
Lee, Mike	2009-12	Martinson, Steve	1977-81	Moore, Jerry	1968-71	Oster, Bob	1972-73
Lehto, Harold	1936-39	Marvin, Aaron	2007-11	Moore, Terry	1966-67	Ouimet, Nick	1997-98
Lehun, Jonathan	2002-03	Matanich, Tom	1973-74	Moreland, Jake	1999-03		
Leitza, Brian	1994-98	Matchinsky, John	1982-87	Morley, David	2011-	Paepke, Mark	1984-85
Lempe, Todd	1981-83	Maus, Robert	1931-32	Moser, Jay	1991-93	Paglarini, Armand	1939-40
Leonard, Tom	1966-67	McClellan, Rich	1968-69	Mosey, Tony	2007-11	Paige, Bob	1958-59
Lepler, P.J.	1992-96	McCormack, Brian	2002-04	Motzko, Bob	1984-86	Palm, Doug	1973-75
LeRoy, Mike	1950-51	McDonald, Brendan	1951-53	Motzko, Joe	1999-03	Pansiro, Hank	1950-52
Lerum, Marty	1969-71	McElroy, T.J.	2002-06	Muir, Ron	1974-77	Papa, Ryan	2013-
Lescarreau, Tony	1953-54	McFarlane, Tom	1976-79	Murphy, Thomas	1931-32	Paradise, Dave	1993-97
Leysring, Tony	1983-84	McGonagle, Phil	1951-52	Murray, Jimmy	2012-	Pariseau, Dale	1968-69
Lideen, Tim	1995-98	McGowan, Ed	1959-60			Parker, Herb	1955-56
Lievers, Brett	1990-95	McGowan, Pat	1987-91	Nelson, Bernard	1932-33	Parrish, Geno	1996-00
Lind, Tom	1972-76	McKay, Pete	1968-72	Nelson, Bruce	1965-66	Parrish, Mark	1995-97
Lindbohm, John	1951-54	McKinley, Brian	1962-64	Nelson, Gary	1966-67	Pascuzzi, Phil	1969-72
Lindgren, Charlie	2013-	McKnight, Kerry	1971-72	Nevalainen, Niklas	2013-	Passolt, Jeff	1977-81
Linn, Bob	1967-68	McLaughlin, Kyle	1995-99	Niedzielski, Ron	1957-59	Paulson, Altin	1961-64
Linsay, Howie	1954-55	McLean, Dave	1979-82	Nierengarten, Will	1932-33	Payne, Al	1968-70
Lobdell, Robert	1933-35	McLean, John	1976-78	Noble, Ed	1960-62	Pearson, Bruce	1960-61
Lodahl, Kris	1986-88	McNamara, Jim	2001-02	Noble, Terry	1962-63	Pearson, Mel	1953-56
Lodermeier, Edwin	1931-33	McVey, Bernie	1972-73	Nodl, Andreas	2006-08	Pearson, Ralph	1941-42
Lovdahl, Bill	1979-81	McWhirter, Ben	1937-40	Noga, Matt	1996-00	Peart, Tom	1977-82
Luger, Bille	2003-04	Meier, Jerry	1971-72	Nordine, Brian	1972-74	Peckskamp, Ryan	2006-10
Lund, Bill	1992-95	Melbourne, Ryan	2001-02	Nornberg, Alfred	1934-35	Perrault, Mark	1981-83
Lund, Tom	1996-00	Melson, Taj	1992-96	Notermann, Mike	1987-91	Perron, Dave	1973-76
Lundberg, Kenneth	1934-35	Melstrom, Ed	1953-55	Novaczyk, Todd	1968-69	Peters, Colin	2000-04
Lundbohm, Andy	2000-04	Mendel, Jay	1979-83	Novak, Travis	2008-12	Peterson, Gary	1971-73
Lutz, Gary	1976-77	Mendel, Jon	1984-86			Peterson, Joel	2001-02
Lyerly, Ethan	2004-05	Mertzacher, John	1931-32	Oas, Bill	1963-64	Pfannenstein, Chuck	1954-55
		Mesenbourg, Mike	1977-78	Oberstar, Paul	1969-71	Pfannenstein, Dave	1979-83
Maas, Leroy	1935-36	Meyer, Charlie	1974-77	O'Brien, B.J.	2006-08	Phillippi, Joe	2011-

Pickett, Rod	1959-62	Rioux, Nicholas	2008-11	Schopf, Dick	1978-79	Talafous, Bob	1983-84
Pietruszewski, Mark	1978-82	Robertson, Gordy	1969-71	Schultz, William	1950-52	Tam, Greg	2002-04
Platzer, Bruce	1971-72	Rodak, Adam	1993-96	Schuman, Kurt	1973-74	Tapp, John	1967-68
Pojar, Jon	1990-92	Roe, Garrett	2007-11	Schuster, Brian	2000-03	Taslo, Bill	1980-81
Poznik, Don	1954-56	Rokola, Jim	1988-89	Scott, Ed	1952-53	Tauer, Greg	1972-74
Poznik, Roy	1954-58	Rolle, Bernard	1939-40	Shannon, Mike	1965-69	Taylor, Lefty	1952-53
Pratt, Dan	1980-84	Rollins, Al	1966-67	Sherman, John	1957-58	Tedesco, Daniel	2013-
Priola, Shannon	1970-71	Roney, Dwayne	1968-69	Shermoen, Craig	1987-89	Terrahe, Peter	1955-56
Prochno, Andrew	2011-	Roos, Dave	1976-80	Sherry, Tim	1961-62	Tharaldson, John	1987-91
Prohaska, Gert	1998-99	Rootes, Tim	1972-73	Shimmon, Bill	1948-50	Thauwald, Jeff	1958-59
Proulx, Jim	1969-71	Rosequist, John	1947-49	Singer, Josh	2004-06	Thielman, Frank	1931-33
Prow, Ethan	2012-	Ross, Steve	1989-93	Sjerven, Grant	1991-94	Thompson, Scott	1973-75
Puckett, Karl	1983-84	Rotsch, Jim	1963-66	Skaja, Ron	1984-86	Thompson, Terry	1970-72
Pudlick, Mike	1998-00	Rucinski, Mike	1996-99	Skinner, John	1971-74	Thorp, Gary	1961-63
Pulczinske, Cril	1950-51	Rutherford, Jim	1954-58	Smith, Curt	1970-73	Thorson, Cory	2010-14
Purslow, Chris	1999-01	Rutten, Roger	1972-76	Songle, Denny	1961-63	Tollette, Jeff	1984-86
		Ryan, Mitch	2008-10	Souders, Charles	1949-50	Toninato, Reid	1972-73
Quist, Duane	1950-53			Splinter, Tom	1973-75	Toninato, Rick	1970-72
		Saatzer, Randy	1974-75	St. Martin, Tim	1984-87	Torsson, Peter	1997-00
Rabey, Jared	2011-	Saatzer, Randy	1947-49	Stanius, Harry	1961-63	Townsend, Joey	1960-61
Raboin, Garrett	2006-10	Sachen, George	1947-48	Stefano, Gary	1977-81	Tuomie, Tray	1986-88
Raduns, Nate	2003-07	Salpacka, Arthur	1934-36	Steichen, Francis	1940-42	Turene, Ed	1954-56
Rahn, Noel	1991-93	Sampair, Brandon	1997-01	Steichen, Woodrow	1937-39	Turgeon, Mike	1980-83
Ramberg, Chris	1991-93	Santerre, Gino	1991-95	Steidl, Matt	1973-77	Tweeton, Tom	1953-54
Randolph, Doug	1977-78	Sarsland, Terry	1969-70	Steinkopf, Tim	1979-83	Tykeson, John	1994-96
Rasmussen, Jim	1973-74	Sarsland, Tony	1968-69	Stephenson, Matt	2004-08	
Ratsch, Jim	1963-66	Saterdalen, Jeff	1988-92	Stewart, Brett	1990-91	Uhrbom, Morris	1940-42
Reed, Rian	1983-87	Sauer, Cosmos	1941-42	Stewart, Jason	1994-98	
Reeder, Konrad	2002-06	Sauter, Pat	1967-69	Stone, Dave	1990-95	Vadies, George	1957-58
Regan, Jeff	1983-84	Sayovitz, Joe	1938-39	Storm, Ben	2013-	Vandell, Ben	1936-38
Rehkamp, Joe	2011-	Schaefer, Dave	1962-63	Strand, Dave	1947-48	Vandell, Roland	1933-35
Reichel, Dave	1976-79	Schaefer, Joe	1971-72	Strobel, Clifford	1931-32	Vannelli, Mike	1984-87
Reichel, Jerry	1952-55	Schaefer, Keith	1954-57	Sullivan, John	1983-84	Vekich, Derek	1987-88
Reichel, Mark	1977-80	Scheid, Chris	1987-91	Sullivan, Mike	1966-67	Vicari, Andy	1994-98
Reid, Cam	2010-12	Scherek, Randy	1973-76	Sullivan, Pat	1973-75	Volpei, Brian	2007-11
Reijola, Rasmus	2012-	Schipper, Phil	1972-73	Svendsen, Dave	1961-63	Vukson, Miles	1940-42
Reimann, Dan	1992-96	Schlink, Jeff	1976-80	Swan, Dan	1983-84	
Reimers, Jason	2002-03	Schmalzbauer, Tony	1986-90	Swanson, John	2005-09	Wahlers, Fred	1967-71
Remitz, Duke	1985-86	Schmidt, Jeff	1991-95	Swarthout, Earl	1940-42	Wallin, Scott	1978-79
Renslow, David	1967-70	Schmidt, Jerry	1985-87	Swarthout, Ralph	1952-56	Wallin, Yard	1983-84
Rieder, Kelly	1992-96	Schneider, Dan	1977-80	Szabo, Peter	2001-05	Walsh, Mike	1999-03
Ries, Bill	1982-86	Scholtmuller, Jerry	1954-55	Tabor, Bill	1977-79	Warren, Jimmy	1941-42

Weasler, Dean	1998-02
Weber, David	1950-51
Weber, Gerry	1962-64
Weida, Robby	1981-84
Weslosky, Jase	2006-09
Westcott, Duvie	1999-01
Weston, Sheldon	1981-84
Whalers, Fred	1967-71
Whitbred, Charles	1971-72
Whitloff, Larry	1959-62
Wick, Jay	1985-86
Wick, Tim	1971-75
Williams, Dick	1968-69
Williams, Tom	1976-77
Wingate, Jordy	1988-92
Winter, Cletus	1933-35
Witucki, Steve	1985-88
Woebkenberg, Paul	1970-71
Wolter, Jordan	1981-84
Wright, Nate	2002-04
Wright, Perry	1960-61
Wuotila, Randolph	1940-41
Yelle, Jim	1982-84
Yerxa, Dennis	1956-58
Yohnke, Mike	1978-79
Zabkowicz, Sam	2008-12
Zaleski, Chris	1997-98
Zanoni, Bob	1948-49
Zanoni, Rudy	1939-40
Zittlow, Gary	1966-68

Notable Supporters
Of SCSU Hockey Program

Anne Abicht	Brendan McDonald
Kevin Allenspach	Joe Meierhofer
Dr. Sue Becker	Jeremiah Minkel
Bob Bess	Tom Nelson
Taryl Clark	Bernie Omann
Chuck Clausen	Dr. Earl Potter III
Chris Coburn	Bill and Sue Prout
Tracy Dill	William Radovich
Marcia Elwell	Leroy Radovich
Gino Gasparini	Roy Saigo
Bruce Grube	Holly Schmidtbauer
Mick Hatten	Mike Schnettler
Dr. William Hudson	Brian Schoenborn
Husky Club	Marty Sundvall
Bill Kemp	Kurt Stelten
Mike Killeen	Therese Todd
Bill and Sheila Kloeppner	George and Shirley Torrey
Dr. Morris Kurtz	Heather Weems
Bob LaCroix	St. Cloud Times
Steve Ludwig	Suzie Williams
Don Lyons	Sean LaFavor
Del Matteson	The Dog Pound

Center Ice Club

St. Cloud State University

HERB BROOKS AND BRENDAN MCDONALD

TOM NELSON

(L-R) MATT CHAPMAN, GARRETT RABOIN, HEATHER WEEMS, BOB MOTZKO, JEFF GIESEN, DREW LEBLANC,
TOM NELSON, EARL POTTER, JOEL LARSEN, BRYAN DEMAINE, JEREMIAH MINKEL, SUE PROUT, BILL PROUT

TRAVIS ZINS

BLIZZARD

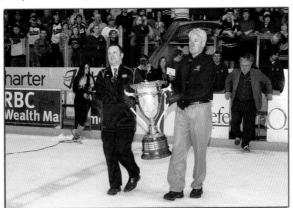

JEREMIAH MINKEL

ERIK HALVERSON AND JOE MEIERHOFFER

WILLIAM RADOVICH AND STEVE LUDWIG TALKING TO A PLAYER

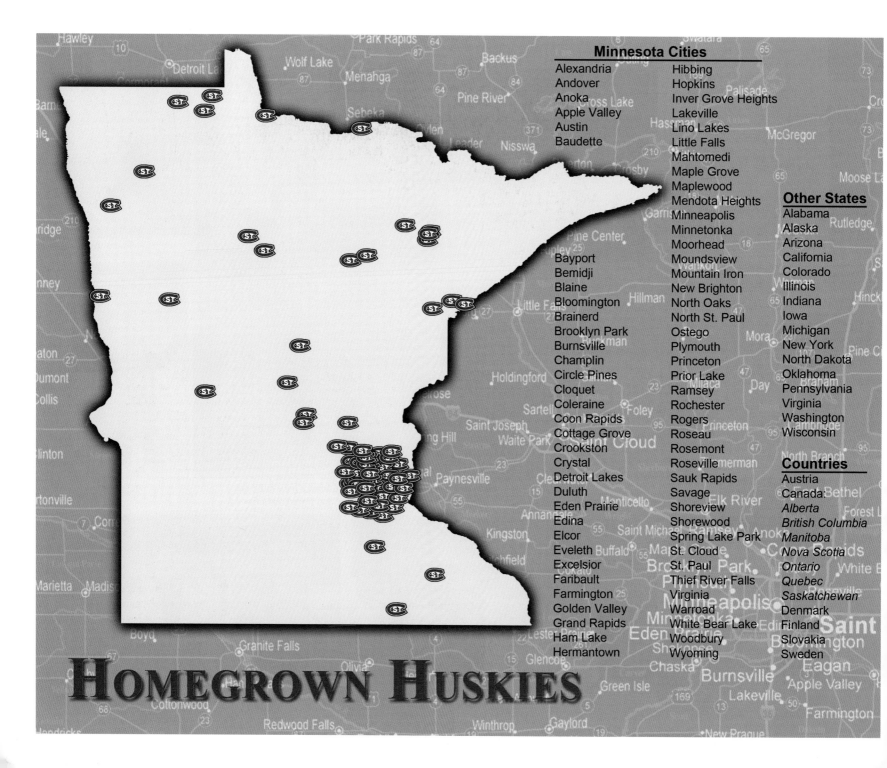

Minnesota Cities

Alexandria	Hibbing
Andover	Hopkins
Anoka	Inver Grove Heights
Apple Valley	Lakeville
Austin	Lino Lakes
Baudette	Little Falls
	Mahtomedi
	Maple Grove
	Maplewood
	Mendota Heights
	Minneapolis
	Minnetonka
	Moorhead
Bayport	Moundsview
Bemidji	Mountain Iron
Blaine	New Brighton
Bloomington	North Oaks
Brainerd	North St. Paul
Brooklyn Park	Ostego
Burnsville	Plymouth
Champlin	Princeton
Circle Pines	Prior Lake
Cloquet	Ramsey
Coleraine	Rochester
Coon Rapids	Rogers
Cottage Grove	Roseau
Crookston	Rosemont
Crystal	Roseville
Detroit Lakes	Sauk Rapids
Duluth	Savage
Eden Prairie	Shoreview
Edina	Shorewood
Elcor	Spring Lake Park
Eveleth	St. Cloud
Excelsior	St. Paul
Faribault	Thief River Falls
Farmington	Virginia
Golden Valley	Warroad
Grand Rapids	White Bear Lake
Ham Lake	Woodbury
Hermantown	Wyoming

Other States

Alabama
Alaska
Arizona
California
Colorado
Illinois
Indiana
Iowa
Michigan
New York
North Dakota
Oklahoma
Pennsylvania
Virginia
Washington
Wisconsin

Countries

Austria
Canada:
Alberta
British Columbia
Manitoba
Nova Scotia
Ontario
Quebec
Saskatchewan
Denmark
Finland
Slovakia
Sweden

HOMEGROWN HUSKIES

ABOUT THE AUTHOR

Marty Mjelleli graduated Cum Laude from St. Cloud State University with a double major in Business Marketing and Communication Studies. During his time with the Huskies from 2004-08, he played on very talented teams that went to the WCHA Final 5 three times and twice to the NCAA tournament. Marty was a three time WCHA All-Academic team member, earned 2008 NCAA Hockey Humanitarian recognition, and was a finalist for the Lowe's Senior Class All-American Award. After his days of being a Husky, Marty played professional hockey for the Johnstown Chiefs of the East Coast Hockey League and played in Europe for the Amsterdam Tigers. He also was a head coach in the USHL for the Des Moines Buccaneers. A hockey enthusiast himself, author Marty Mjelleli wanted to preserve the vivid history of Husky hockey through vintage photos, stats and stories. Marty met his wife Shannon at SCSU; they currently reside in Bloomington, MN.

ACKNOWLEDGMENTS AND DEDICATIONS

This book was made possible through the contributions of many individuals. I am very appreciative of SCSU and the staff that provided valuable of material; Anne Abicht and Tom Nelson were exceptionally helpful. SCSU alum Sean LaFavor for his masterful journalism and editing assistance. The fantastic pictures were provided by photographers Neil Andersen, Brace Hemmelgarn, and archivist Tom Steman. Graphics and computer work were created by my talented step-dad, Jeff Lorenzen. I would also like to thank the NCHC, WCHA, NHL teams, IIHF, and USA hockey for their cooperation. A special thanks to the players and other individuals that shared their stories.

I want to dedicate this book to all my teammates. The coaching staff of Bob Motzko and Craig Dahl; your relentless pursuit of making Husky hockey a perennial power makes alumni proud. Thank you to the fans that make St. Cloud truly a special place. To Shattuck St. Mary's and the Des Moines Buccaneers for giving me a platform to earn a NCAA scholarship. I am grateful for the mentors who have all had a tremendous impact on my career; Bob Ferguson, Tom Ward, and J.P. Parise. My friends and family that have been an incredible influence in my life; my wife Shannon, brother Mario, and parents Terry and Marty Sr. who taught me the meaning of "Never be Content".